"LET ME SAY, AT THE RISK OF
SEEMING RIDICULOUS, THAT THE
TRUE REVOLUTIONARY IS GUIDED BY
GREAT FEELINGS OF LOVE."

ERNESTO CHE GUEVARA

"CHE SYMBOLIZES NOT SELLING OUT, STAYING TRUE TO WHAT YOU BELIEVE IN." —BENICIO DEL TORO

"CHE'S LIFE IS AN INSPIRATION FOR EVERY HUMAN BEING WHO LOVES FREEDOM." —NELSON MANDELA

"IN THESE PRESENT TIMES, WHEN FOR MANY ETHICS AND OTHER PROFOUND MORAL VALUES ARE SEEN TO BE SO EASILY BOUGHT AND SOLD, THE EXAMPLE OF CHE GUEVARA TAKES ON AN EVEN GREATER DIMENSION." —RIGOBERTA MENCHU

"THE POWERFUL OF THE EARTH SHOULD TAKE HEED: DEEP INSIDE THAT T-SHIRT WHERE WE HAVE TRIED TO TRAP HIM, THE EYES OF CHE GUEVARA ARE STILL BURNING WITH IMPATIENCE." —ARIEL DORFMAN

"CHE IS SOMEONE WE WILL NEVER TRULY FATHOM BECAUSE HIS ENLIGHTENMENT ON THE SUFFERING OF OTHERS, AND HIS DEDICATION TO ENDING THAT SUFFERING, WILL ALWAYS SEEM MYSTERIOUS TO US, WHO ON MOST DAYS CANNOT EVEN IMAGINE THE EQUANIMITY OF HIS INNER FREEDOM." —ALICE WALKER

"CHE WAS THE MOST COMPLETE HUMAN BEING OF OUR AGE." —JEAN-PAUL SARTRE

"THERE WAS NO PERSON MORE FEARED BY THE COMPANY [CIA] THAN CHE GUEVARA BECAUSE HE HAD THE CAPACITY AND CHARISMA NECESSARY TO DIRECT THE STRUGGLE AGAINST THE POLITICAL REPRESSION OF THE TRADITIONAL HIERARCHIES IN POWER IN THE COUNTRIES OF LATIN AMERICA." —PHILIP AGEE, FORMER CIA AGENT

"THERE ARE PEOPLE WHO CARRY INSIDE THEM THE DIGNITY OF THE WORLD, AND ONE OF THOSE IS CHE." —FIDEL CASTRO

ERNESTO CHE GUEVARA

CHE

THE DIARIES OF
ERNESTO CHE GUEVARA

THE BASIS OF THE MOVIE
CHE
FROM STEVEN SODERBERGH
AND BENICIO DEL TORO

Ocean Press

Melbourne ▪ New York
www.oceanbooks.com.au

ISBN 978-1-920888-93-0
Library of Congress Catalog Card Number: 2008910124

First Printed 2009
Printed in the USA

PUBLISHED BY OCEAN PRESS

E-mail: info@oceanbooks.com.au
Australia: GPO Box 3279, Melbourne, Victoria 3001, Australia
USA: 511 Avenue of the Americas, #96, New York, NY 10011-8436, USA

OCEAN PRESS TRADE DISTRIBUTORS

United States and Canada: **Consortium Book Sales and Distribution**
                          Tel: 1-800-283-3572 www.cbsd.com
Australia and New Zealand: **Palgrave Macmillan**
                          E-mail: customer.service@macmillan.com.au
Mexico and Latin America: **Ocean Sur**
                          E-mail: info@oceansur.com

www.oceanbooks.com.au
info@oceanbooks.com.au

CONTENTS

PART TWO: GUERRILLA

FURTHER READING

ERNESTO CHE GUEVARA

One of *Time* magazine's "icons of the century," Ernesto Guevara de la Serna was born in Rosario, Argentina, on June 14, 1928. He made several trips around Latin America during and immediately after his studies at medical school in Buenos Aires, including his 1952 journey with Alberto Granado, on the unreliable Norton motorbike described in his earlier journal *The Motorcycle Diaries*.

He was already becoming involved in political activity and living in Guatemala when, in 1954, the elected government of Jacobo Árbenz was overthrown in a CIA-organized military operation. Ernesto escaped to Mexico, profoundly radicalized.

Following up on a contact made in Guatemala, Guevara sought out the group of exiled Cuban revolutionaries in Mexico City. In July 1955, he met Fidel Castro and immediately enlisted in the guerrilla expedition to overthrow Cuban dictator Fulgencio Batista. The Cubans nicknamed him "Che," a popular form of address in Argentina.

On November 25, 1956, Guevara set sail for Cuba aboard the yacht *Granma* as the doctor to the guerrilla group that began the revolutionary armed struggle in Cuba's Sierra Maestra mountains. Within several months, he was appointed by Fidel Castro as the first Rebel Army commander, though he continued ministering medically to wounded guerrilla fighters and captured soldiers from Batista's army.

In September 1958, Guevara played a decisive role in the military defeat of Batista after he and Camilo Cienfuegos led separate guerrilla columns westward from the Sierra Maestra described in this book.

After Batista fled on January 1, 1959, Guevara became a key leader of the new revolutionary government, first as head of the Department of Industry of the National Institute of Agrarian Reform; then as president of the National Bank. In February 1961 he became minister of industry. He was also a central leader of the political organization that in 1965 became the Communist Party of Cuba.

Apart from these responsibilities, Guevara represented the Cuban revolutionary government around the world, heading numerous delegations and speaking at the United Nations and other international forums in Asia, Africa, Latin America, and the socialist bloc countries. He earned a reputation as a passionate and articulate spokesperson for Third World peoples, most famously at the conference at Punta del Este in Uruguay, where he denounced US President Kennedy's Alliance for Progress.

As had been his intention since joining the Cuban revolutionary movement, Guevara left Cuba in April 1965, initially to lead a Cuban-organized guerrilla mission to support the revolutionary struggle in the Congo, Africa. He returned to Cuba secretly in December 1965, to prepare another Cuban-organized guerrilla force for Bolivia. Arriving in Bolivia in November 1966, Guevara's plan was to challenge that country's military dictatorship and eventually to instigate a revolutionary movement that would extend throughout the continent of Latin America. The journal he kept during the Bolivian campaign became known as *The Bolivian Diary*. Che was wounded and captured by US-trained and run Bolivian counterinsurgency troops on October 8, 1967. The following day he was murdered and his body hidden.

Che Guevara's remains were finally discovered in 1997 and returned to Cuba. A memorial was built at Santa Clara in central Cuba, where he had won a major military battle during the revolutionary war.

"LET THE FLAG UNDER WHICH WE FIGHT BE THE SACRED CAUSE OF HUMANITY."

★

ERNESTO CHE GUEVARA

CHRONOLOGY OF ERNESTO CHE GUEVARA

June 14, 1928 Ernesto Guevara is born in Rosario, Argentina, of parents Ernesto Guevara Lynch and Celia de la Serna; he will be the eldest of five children.

January–July 1952 Ernesto Guevara travels around Latin America with his friend Alberto Granado.

March 10, 1952 General Fulgencio Batista carries out a coup d'état in Cuba.

July 6, 1953 After graduating as a doctor in March, Ernesto Guevara sets off again to travel through Latin America. He visits Bolivia, observing the aftermath of the 1952 revolution.

July 26, 1953 Fidel Castro leads an unsuccessful armed attack on the Moncada army garrison in Santiago de Cuba, launching the revolutionary struggle to overthrow the Batista regime.

December 1953 Ernesto Guevara meets a group of Cuban survivors of the Moncada attack in San José, Costa Rica.

December 24, 1953 Ernesto Guevara arrives in Guatemala, then under the popularly elected government of Jacobo Árbenz.

January–June 1954 While in Guatemala, he studies Marxism and becomes involved in political activities, meeting exiled Cuban revolutionaries.

August 1954 Mercenary troops backed by the CIA enter Guatemala City and begin massacring Árbenz supporters.

September 21, 1954 Ernesto Guevara arrives in Mexico City after fleeing Guatemala. He gets a job at the Central Hospital.

July 1955 Ernesto Guevara meets Fidel Castro soon after the latter arrives in exile in Mexico City after his release from prison in Cuba. Che immediately agrees to join the planned guerrilla expedition to Cuba. The Cubans nickname him "Che," an Argentine term of greeting.

June 24, 1956 Che is arrested as part of a roundup by Mexican police of exiled Cuban revolutionaries.

November 25, 1956 Eighty-two combatants, including Che Guevara as troop doctor, sail for Cuba from Tuxpan, Mexico, aboard the small cabin cruiser *Granma*.

December 2, 1956 The *Granma* reaches Cuba at Las Coloradas beach in Oriente province but are surprised by Batista's troops at Alegría de Pío and dispersed.

December 21, 1956 Che's group (led by Juan Almeida) reunites with Fidel Castro and his group, and they move deeper into the Sierra Maestra mountains.

January 17, 1957 The Rebel Army with some new peasant recruits successfully takes an army outpost in the battle of La Plata.

January 22, 1957 A significant victory over Batista's forces is scored at Arroyo del Infierno.

February 17, 1957 *New York Times* journalist Herbert Matthews interviews Fidel Castro in the Sierra Maestra. The same day, the first meeting is held between the urban underground and the guerrillas of the July 26 Movement since the start of the revolutionary war.

March 13, 1957 A group of students from the Revolutionary Directorate attack the Presidential Palace and seize a major Havana radio station. Student leader José Antonio Echeverría is killed in this attack.

May 27–28, 1957 The battle of El Uvero takes place, in which Che Guevara stands out among the combatants.

July 12, 1957 The rebels issue the Manifesto of the Sierra Maestra calling for a broad political front against General Batista and support for the Rebel Army.

July 21, 1957 Che Guevara is selected to lead the newly established second column (Column 4) of the Rebel Army and is promoted to the rank of commander.

July 30, 1957 Frank País, the young leader of the urban underground in Santiago de Cuba, is killed.

August 20, 1957 Fidel leads Column 1 (José Martí) in defeating Batista's forces in the battle of Palma Mocha.

September 17, 1957 Che's forces ambush army troops at Pino del Agua.

October, 1957 The rebels establish a permanent supply base at El Hombrito in the Sierra Maestra.

October 12, 1957 Batista launches a brutal campaign to destroy the Rebel Army in the Sierra Maestra.

November–December, 1957 The rebels respond with a "winter offensive" against Batista's army.

February 16-17, 1958 The Rebel Army wins a significant victory against Batista in the second battle of Pino del Agua.

March 1, 1958 Raúl Castro and Juan Almeida lead columns that open up second and third fronts in Oriente province.

April 9, 1958 A national general strike is defeated.

May 25, 1958 Batista launches a military offensive against the Rebel Army, but this fails after two and a half months of intensive fighting.

July 11–21, 1958 A decisive defeat is inflicted on Batista's army in the battle of El Jigüe, significantly expanding the rebels' operational zone in the Sierra Maestra.

August 31, 1958 Che Guevara and Camilo Cienfuegos lead invasion columns west from the Sierra Maestra toward central Cuba, opening new battle fronts in Las Villas province.

November 15, 1958 Fidel leaves the Sierra Maestra to direct the Rebel Army's final offensive in Santiago de Cuba. By the end of the month, Batista's elite troops are defeated at the battle of Guisa.

December 28, 1958 Che Guevara's Column 8 initiates the battle of Santa Clara and succeeds in taking control of the city within a few days.

January 1, 1959 Batista flees Cuba. Fidel enters Santiago de Cuba as the military regime collapses. Santa Clara falls to the Rebel Army.

January 2, 1959 Fidel Castro calls for a general strike and the country is paralyzed. The Rebel Army columns led by Che Guevara and Camilo Cienfuegos reach Havana.

January 8, 1959 Fidel Castro arrives in Havana.

February 9, 1959 Che Guevara is declared a Cuban citizen.

June 12–September 8, 1959 Che Guevara travels through Europe, Africa, and Asia; he signs various commercial, technical, and cultural agreements on behalf of the revolutionary government.

October 7, 1959 Che Guevara is designated head of the Department of Industry of the National Institute of Agrarian Reform (INRA).

November 25, 1959 Che Guevara is appointed president of the National Bank of Cuba.

March 5, 1960 At the funeral for the victims of a terrorist bombing on board the French ship *La Coubre*, Cuban photographer Alberto Korda snaps his famous photograph of Che Guevara.

March 17, 1960 President Eisenhower approves a CIA plan to overthrow the revolutionary government and to train a Cuban exile army to invade Cuba.

October 21, 1960 Che Guevara leaves on an extended visit to the Soviet Union, the German Democratic Republic, Czechoslovakia, China, and North Korea.

January 3, 1961 Washington breaks diplomatic relations with Cuba.

February 23, 1961 The revolutionary government establishes the Ministry of Industry, headed by Che Guevara.

April 15, 1961 As a prelude to the planned invasion by US-organized forces, planes attack Santiago de Cuba and Havana.

April 16, 1961 At a mass rally Fidel Castro proclaims the socialist character of the Cuban revolution.

April 17-19, 1961 One thousand five hundred Cuban-born mercenaries, organized and backed by the United States, invade Cuba at the Bay of Pigs but are defeated within 72 hours. Che Guevara is sent to command troops in Pinar del Río province.

August 8, 1961 Che Guevara condemns US President Kennedy's "Alliance for Progress" in a fiery speech to Organization of American States (OAS) Economic and Social Conference in Punta del Este, Uruguay, as head of Cuba's delegation. Cuba is subsequently expelled from the OAS.

February 3, 1962 President Kennedy orders a total trade embargo against Cuba.

August 27–September 7, 1962 Che Guevara makes his second visit to the Soviet Union.

October 1962 An international crisis breaks out after US spy planes discover Soviet missile installations in Cuba. Cuba responds by mobilizing its population for defense. Che Guevara is assigned to lead forces in Pinar del Río province in preparation for an imminent US invasion.

July 3–17, 1963 Che Guevara visits Algeria, recently independent under the government of Ahmed Ben Bella.

March 1964 Che Guevara meets with Tamara Bunke (Tania) to discuss her mission to move to Bolivia in anticipation of a future guerrilla expedition.

March 25, 1964 Che Guevara addresses the UN Conference on Trade and Development in Geneva, Switzerland.

November 4–9, 1964 Che Guevara visits the Soviet Union.

December 11, 1964 Che Guevara addresses the UN General Assembly meeting in New York, condemning the US war in Vietnam and supporting independence movements from Puerto Rico to the Congo.

December 17, 1964 Che Guevara leaves New York for Africa, where he visits Algeria, Mali, Congo (Brazzaville), Guinea, Ghana, Tanzania, and Egypt.

February 24, 1965 Che Guevara addresses the Second Economic Seminar of the Organization of Afro-Asian Solidarity in Algiers, controversially urging the socialist countries to do more to support Third World struggles for independence.

March 14, 1965 Che Guevara returns to Cuba and shortly afterwards drops from public view.

April 1, 1965 Che Guevara delivers a farewell letter to Fidel Castro. He subsequently leaves Cuba on a Cuban-sponsored internationalist mission in the Congo, Africa, entering through Tanzania.

April 18, 1965 In answer to questions about Che Guevara's whereabouts, Fidel Castro tells foreign reporters that Che "will always be where he is most useful to the revolution."

June 16, 1965 Fidel Castro announces Che Guevara's location will be revealed "when Commander Guevara wants it known."

October 3, 1965 Fidel Castro publicly reads Che Guevara's letter of farewell at a meeting to announce the central committee of the newly formed Communist Party of Cuba.

November 21, 1965 Che Guevara leaves the Congo, and begins writing up his account of the African mission, which he describes as a "failure."

December 1965 Fidel Castro arranges for Che Guevara to return to Cuba in secret. Che Guevara prepares for a Cuban-sponsored guerrilla expedition to Bolivia.

January 3–14, 1966 The Tricontinental Conference of Solidarity of the Peoples of Asia, Africa, and Latin America is held in Havana.

March 1966 The first Cuban combatants arrive in Bolivia to begin advance preparations for a guerrilla movement. Tania has already been working there since 1964.

July 1966 Che Guevara meets with Cuban volunteers selected for the mission to Bolivia at a training camp in Cuba's Pinar del Río province.

November 4, 1966 Che Guevara arrives in La Paz, Bolivia, in disguise, using the assumed name of Ramón Benítez.

November 7, 1966 Che Guevara and several others arrive at the farm on the Ñacahuazú River where the guerrilla detachment will be based. Che makes his first entry in his diary of the Bolivia campaign.

December 31, 1966 Che Guevara meets with the secretary of the Bolivian Communist Party, Mario Monje. There is disagreement over perspectives for the planned guerrilla movement.

March 23, 1967 The first guerrilla military action takes place in a successful ambush of Bolivian Army troops.

March 25, 1967 The formation of the Bolivian National Liberation Army (ELN) is publicly announced.

April 16, 1967 Publication of Che Guevara's "Message to the Tricontinental," which calls for the creation of "two, three, many Vietnams."

April 17, 1967 The guerrilla detachment led by Joaquín (Vilo Acuña) is separated from the rest of the unit. The separation is supposed to last only a few days but the two groups are never able to reunite.

April 20, 1967 French intellectual Regís Debray and Ciro Bustos are arrested after having spent several weeks with the guerrilla unit in Bolivia. They are subsequently tried and sentenced to 30 years' imprisonment.

May 1967 US Special Forces arrive in Bolivia to train counterinsurgency troops of the Bolivian Army.

June 23-24, 1967 The Bolivian Army massacres miners and their families at the Siglo XX mines. This becomes known as the San Juan massacre.

June 26, 1967 The guerrillas ambush army troops at Florida.

July 1, 1967 President Barrientos publicly announces Che Guevara's presence in Bolivia.

July 6, 1967 The guerrillas occupy the town of Sumaipata.

July 26, 1967 Che addresses the guerrilla troops on the significance of the July 26, 1953, attack on the Moncada garrison.

July 31–August 10, 1967 The Organization of Latin American Solidarity (OLAS) conference is held in Havana. The conference supports guerrilla movements throughout Latin America. Che Guevara is elected honorary chair.

August 4, 1967 A deserter leads the Bolivian Army to the guerrilla's main supply cache. Documents discovered there lead to the arrest of key urban contacts.

August 31, 1967 Joaquín's detachment, which includes Tania, is ambushed and annihilated while crossing the Río Grande at Puerto Mauricio (Vado del Yeso).

September 14, 1967 Loyola Guzmán is arrested along with hundreds of others suspected of collaborating with the guerrilla movement.

September 22, 1967 The guerrillas occupy the town of Alto Seco.

September 26, 1967 The guerrilla unit falls into a Bolivian Army ambush at Quebrada de Batán, near La Higuera.

October 8, 1967 The remaining 17 guerrillas are trapped by army troops and conduct a desperate battle in the Quebrada del Yuro (El Yuro ravine). Che Guevara is seriously wounded and captured.

October 9, 1967 Che Guevara and two other captured guerrillas (Willy and Chino) are murdered by Bolivian soldiers following instructions from the Bolivian government and Washington. The remains of Che Guevara and the other guerrillas are secretly buried in Bolivia.

October 14, 1967 Survivors of the battle of Quebrada del Yuro are ambushed at the fork of the Mizque and Río Grande rivers.

October 15, 1967 In a television appearance Fidel Castro confirms news of Che Guevara's death and declares three days of official mourning in Cuba. October 8 is designated the Day of the Heroic Guerrilla.

October 18, 1967 Fidel Castro delivers a memorial speech for Che Guevara in Havana's Revolution Plaza before an audience of almost one million people.

February 22, 1968 Three Cuban survivors (Pombo, Urbano, and Benigno) cross the Bolivian border into Chile, after traveling across the Andes on foot. They succeed in making it back to Cuba. Two Bolivians (Inti and Darío) stay in Bolivia and later reorganize the ELN.

Mid-March 1968 Microfilm of the pages of Che's Bolivian diaries arrives in Cuba.

July 1968 Che Guevara's *Bolivian Diary* is published in Cuba and distributed free of charge to the Cuban people. It is simultaneously published in many countries to counter the CIA campaign to discredit the revolutionary movement in Latin America. With an introduction by Fidel Castro, it becomes an instant international bestseller.

July 1997 Che Guevara's remains are finally located and returned to Cuba and buried along with the bodies of other guerrilla fighters found in Bolivia in a new memorial built in Santa Clara.

MAP OF CUBA 1959

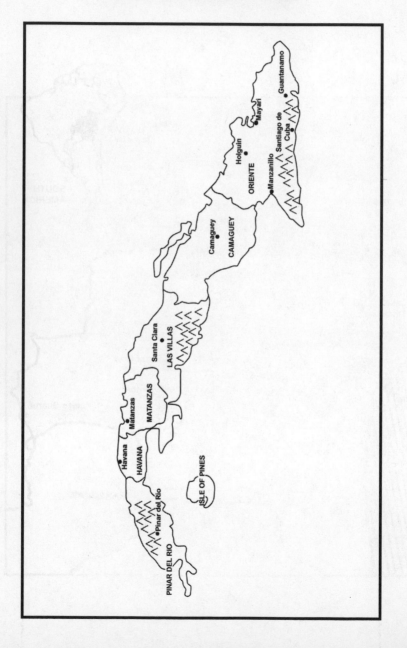

MAP OF BOLIVIA 1966

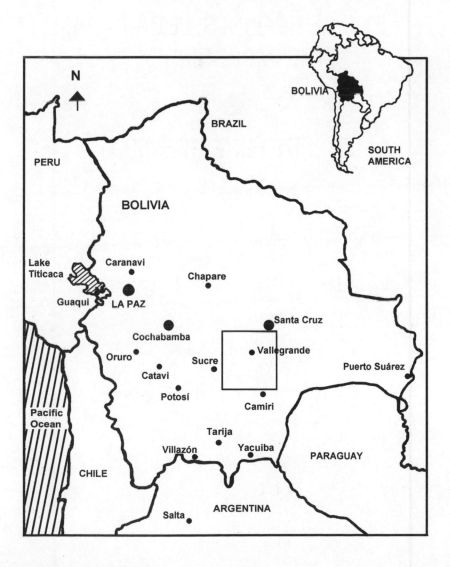

"LET'S BE REALISTS, LET'S DREAM THE IMPOSSIBLE."

★

ERNESTO CHE GUEVARA

PROLOGUE
BY ERNESTO CHE GUEVARA

The stars drew light across the night sky in that little mountain village, and the silence and the cold made the darkness vanish away. It was—I don't know how to explain it—as if everything solid melted away into the ether, eliminating all individuality and absorbing us, rigid, into the immense darkness. Not a single cloud to lend perspective to the space blocked any portion of the starry sky. Less than a few meters away the dim light of a lamp lost its power to fade the darkness.

The man's face was indistinct in the shadows; I could only see what seemed like the spark of his eyes and the gleam of his four front teeth.

I still can't say whether it was the atmosphere or the personality of that individual that prepared me for the revelation, but I know that many times and from many different people I had heard those same arguments and that they had never made an impression on me. Our interlocutor was, in fact, a very interesting character. From a country in Europe, he escaped the knife of dogmatism as a young man, he knew the taste of fear (one of the few experiences which makes you value life), and afterwards he had wandered from country to country, gathering thousands of adventures, until he and his bones finally ended up in this isolated region, patiently waiting for the moment of great reckoning to arrive.

After exchanging a few meaningless words and platitudes, each of us marking territory, the discussion began to falter and we were about to go our separate ways, when he let out his idiosyncratic, childlike laugh, highlighting the asymmetry of his four front incisors:

> The future belongs to the people, and gradually, or in one strike, they will take power, here and in every country.
>
> The terrible thing is the people need to be educated, and this they cannot do before taking power, only after. They can only learn at the cost of their own mistakes, which will be very serious and will cost many innocent lives. Or perhaps not, maybe those lives will not have been innocent because they will have committed the huge sin against nature; meaning, a lack of ability to adapt. All of them, those unable to adapt—you and I, for example—will die cursing the power they helped, through great sacrifice, to create. Revolution is impersonal; it will take their lives, even utilizing their memory as an example or as an instrument for domesticating the youth who follow them. My sin is greater because I, more astute and with greater experience, call it what you like, will die knowing that my sacrifice stems only from an inflexibility symbolizing our rotten civilization, which is crumbling. I also know—and this won't alter the course of history or your personal view of me—that you will die with a clenched fist and a tense jaw, the epitome of hatred and struggle, because you are not a symbol (some inanimate example) but a genuine member of the society to be destroyed; the spirit of the beehive speaks through your mouth and motivates your actions. You are as useful as I am, but you are not aware of how useful your contribution is to the society that sacrifices you.

I saw his teeth and the cheeky grin with which he foretold history, I felt his handshake and, like a distant murmur, his formal goodbye. The night, folding in at contact with his words, overtook me again, enveloping me within it. But despite his words, I now knew... I knew that when the great guiding spirit cleaves humanity into two antagonistic halves, I would be with the people. I know this, I see it printed in the night sky that I, eclectic dissembler of doctrine and psychoanalyst of dogma, howling like one possessed, will assault the barricades or the trenches, will take my bloodstained weapon and, consumed with fury, slaughter any enemy who falls into my hands. And I see, as if a great exhaustion smothers this fresh exaltation, I see myself, immolated in the genuine revolution, the great equalizer of individual will, proclaiming the ultimate mea culpa. I feel my nostrils dilate, savoring the acrid smell of gunpowder and blood, the enemy's death; I steel my body, ready to do battle, and prepare myself to be a sacred space within which the bestial howl of the triumphant proletariat can resound with new energy and new hope.

From: *The Motorcycle Diaries: Notes on a Latin American Journey* by Ernesto Che Guevara.

"THE AMERICAS WILL BE THE THEATER OF MY ADVENTURES IN A WAY THAT IS MUCH MORE SIGNIFICANT THAN I WOULD HAVE BELIEVED."

ERNESTO CHE GUEVARA

(writing to his mother from Guatemala, April 1954)

PART ONE

THE ARGENTINE

THE MOVIE "CHE" (PART 1)

IS BASED ON

REMINISCENCES OF THE CUBAN REVOLUTIONARY WAR

BY ERNESTO CHE GUEVARA

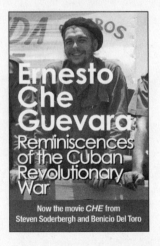

EXCERPTS OF THIS BOOK ARE REPRODUCED HERE

GUATEMALA

D ear old lady,
　　...The latest events belong to history—a quality which I
think is appearing for the first time in my notes. A few days ago,
some aircraft from Honduras crossed the border with Guatemala
and flew over the city in broad daylight, machine gunning people
and military objectives. I enlisted in the health brigades to help on
the medical side and in the youth brigades that patrol the streets
by night. The course of events was as follows. After the aircraft
had passed, troops under the command of Colonel Castillo Armas,
a Guatemalan émigré in Honduras, crossed the frontier at several
points and advanced on the town of Chiquimula. The Guatemalan
government, which had already protested to Honduras, let them
enter without offering any resistance and presented its case to the
United Nations.

　　Colombia and Brazil, two docile Yankee instruments, put forward a plan to pass the matter to the OAS. The Soviet Union re-
jected this and was in favor of ordering a ceasefire. The invaders
failed in their attempt to use aircraft gunfire to get the masses to
rise up, but they did capture the town of Bananera and cut the
railway to Puerto Barrios. The aim of the mercenaries was clear
enough: to take Puerto Barrios and bring in all kinds of weapons

and further mercenary troops. This became apparent when the schooner *Siesta de Trujillo* was captured trying to unload weapons at that port. The final offensive collapsed, but in the midland towns the attackers committed acts of real barbarism, murdering members of SETUFCO [United Fruit Company Workers Union] at the cemetery by throwing a hand grenade at their chests.

The invaders thought that if they just gave a shout, the entire people would come out and follow them — and for this purpose they parachuted in weapons. But in fact the people immediately rallied under the command of [President] Árbenz. The invading troops were checked and defeated on all fronts and driven back past Chiquimula, near the Honduran frontier. Pirate aircraft flying from bases in Honduras and Nicaragua continued to machine-gun the fronts and towns. Chiquimula was heavily bombed, and several people were wounded and a little girl of three killed as a result of the bombing of Guatemala City.

My life has been like this: First I reported to the youth brigades of the Alliance, where I spent several days at a central assembly point until the Health Ministry sent me to be billeted at the Maestro Health Centre. I volunteered for the front, but they didn't pay me a blind bit of notice...

TO MY MOTHER, LATE JUNE 1954

D ear old lady,
A terrible cold shower has fallen on all those who admire Guatemala. On the night of Sunday, June 27, President Árbenz unexpectedly announced that he was resigning. He publicly denounced the [United] Fruit Company and the United States as being directly behind all the bombing and strafing of the civilian population.

An English merchant ship has been bombed and sunk in the

port of San José, and the bombing continues. At this moment Árbenz has announced his decision to place the command in the hands of Colonel Carlos Enrique Díaz. He said that he was motivated by his desire to save the October revolution and to stop the North Americans from coming to this land as masters.

Colonel Díaz said nothing in his speech. The PDR and PRG both expressed their agreement and called on their members to cooperate with the new government. The other two parties, the PRN and the Guatemalan [communist] Labor Party (PGT) said nothing. I went to bed feeling very frustrated about what has happened. I had again spoken to the Health Ministry and asked to be sent to the front. Now I don't know what to do. We'll see what today brings...

Two days thick with political events, although they did not affect me personally. The events: Árbenz resigned under pressure from a North American military mission that was threatening massive bombing and a declaration of war by Honduras and Nicaragua provoking US intervention. But Árbenz may not have foreseen what happened next. On the first day colonels Sánchez and [Elfegio] Monzón (a well-known anticommunist) joined forces with Díaz, and their first decree made the PGT illegal. The persecution began at once and the embassies filled up with people seeking asylum. But worse was to come the next day, when Díaz and Sánchez resigned, leaving Monzón as head of the government with two lieutenant colonels under him. They completely caved in to Castillo Armas (or so it is said), and martial law provisions were decreed for anyone found carrying prohibited calibre weapons. My own situation is roughly that I will be expelled from the small hospital where I am now, probably tomorrow following my reclassification as a "chebol" [Che the Bolshevik]. Repression is coming...

From *Self-Portrait* by Ernesto Che Guevara

"A POLITICAL EVENT WAS MEETING
FIDEL CASTRO, THE CUBAN
REVOLUTIONARY.
HE'S A YOUNG, INTELLIGENT GUY,
VERY SURE OF HIMSELF AND
EXTRAORDINARILY AUDACIOUS; I
THINK WE HIT IT OFF WELL…"

ERNESTO CHE GUEVARA
(writing to his parents, Mexico, August 1955)

MEXICO

After many adventures, I am now established at the general hospital and working quite hard, although in a somewhat disorderly fashion. The food is rather bad for me: if I eat it, I get asthma; if I don't, I go hungry... I now spend my time getting to know the area around Mexico City, together with Hilda [Gadea]. We've been to see some magnificent [Diego] Rivera murals at an agricultural college, and also visited Puebla.

Some good and bad things have been happening. I'm still not sure what my future will be like. Agencia Latina has paid up, but not all of it, and I'll only have 2,000 pesos left to pay some bills and buy some presents. They invited me to the [World] Youth Festival but I would have had to pay my own way; and I was still counting on getting the money I announced to all and sundry that I was planning to go to Spain on July 8. Now it's all come to nothing, and I'm proceeding with my plan to travel around Mexico from September 1. As a sporting event, I should mention the ascent of the lower side of Popocatepetl by a casual group of valiant mountaineers (which included myself). It is wonderful and I would like to do it again fairly often. Pascual Lozano, the Venezuelan, fell behind a little before catching up, even though we took him in tow for the final stage. Another event has been the revolution in Argentina, which fills me with unease because of my brother being in the Marines. The funny event was my invitation to take Hilda and a Peruvian friend to a football game. It got off to a splendid start with lighted mothballs and ended with buckets of shit, which all three of us got.

A political event was that I met Fidel Castro, the Cuban revolutionary. He is a young, intelligent guy, very sure of himself and extraordinarily audacious. I think we hit if off well…

TO MY MOTHER, APPROXIMATELY OCTOBER 1956

Written before leaving for Cuba with the *Granma* expedition.

Dear Mamá,
        Your prickly son, a mean one at that, is not a good-for-nothing; he resembles Paul Muní when he said what he said in a pathetic voice and slipped away into the growing shadows to the strains of music. My current profession is that of a jumping bean — here today, there tomorrow, etc. — which is why I didn't go to see my relatives. (Also, I must confess that it seems to me that I would have more in common with a whale than with a bourgeois couple who are worthy employees of meritorious institutions that I would wipe off the face of the earth if I could. I don't want you to think this is an aversion; it's more like basic distrust, since Lezica has already shown that we speak different languages and have no points of contact.) I've given you this long explanation in parentheses because, after I wrote what precedes it, it seemed to me that you would imagine that I myself was in the process of bourgeoisification. But since I was too lazy to begin again and delete the paragraph, I gave you a lengthy explanation that doesn't look very convincing to me. Full stop. So I'll begin again.

A month from now, Hilda will go to visit her family in Peru, since, rather than a political criminal, she is now considered a somewhat misguided representative of the very worthy anti-communist APRA party. I am in the process of changing the priorities of my studies; previously, for better or worse, I dedicated myself to medicine and spent my free time informally studying St. Karl [Karl Marx]. The new stage of my life also demands a change in priorities: Now, St. Karl comes first — the axis — and will remain so for however many years the spheroid has room for me on its outer mantle; medicine is a more or less amusing diversion, unimportant except for a small area to which I'm thinking of dedicating more than a medullary study, one of those that make the basements of the bookshops tremble under their weight.

As you'll recall, and if you don't remember I'll remind you now, I was working on a book on the role of the doctor, etc., of which I only finished a couple of chapters that whiffed of some pamphlet with a title like *Bodies and Souls*. It was nothing more than badly written rubbish, showing with every step a thorough ignorance of the basics of the subject, so I decided to study. Moreover, to write it, I had to reach a number of conclusions that were kicking against my essentially adventurous trajectory. So I decided to deal with the main things first, to pit myself against the order of things, shield on my arm — the whole fantasy — and then, if the windmills don't break my nut, write more later.

I owe Celia the letter full of praise that I'll write after this one if I have time. The others owe me letters, because I've had the last word with all of them, even Beatriz. Tell her that the newspapers are arriving perfectly and that they give me a very good panoramic view of all the beautiful things the government is doing. I've carefully cut out articles, following my father's example, since Hilda follows that of the mother.

Kisses and whatever should accompany them to all the members of the family, and a response (negative or positive, but nevertheless convincing) on what happened in Guatemala.

Now, only the last part of the speech remains, concerning the little man, which might be called "And What Next?" Now comes the hard part, old lady, what I've never shrunk from and have always enjoyed. The sky hasn't turned black, the constellations haven't left their courses, and there have been no terrible hurricanes or floods; the signs are propitious. They augur victory. But, if they are mistaken — and even the gods make mistakes — I think that, like a poet [Nazim Hikmet] you are not familiar with, I'll be able to say, "I will take to the grave only the **regret** of an unfinished song."

To avoid "pre-mortem" pathos, I won't send this letter until I've burned my boats, and then you'll know that, in a sun-drenched land of the Americas, your son will be cursing himself for not having studied surgery so he could help a wounded man and cursing the Mexican government that didn't let him perfect his already respectable marksmanship so he could knock over targets with greater ease. And the struggle will be waged with our backs to the wall, as in the hymns — until victory or death.

Another kiss for you, with all the affection of a farewell that still resists being total.

Your son.

From *Latin America: Awakening of a Continent* by Ernesto Che Guevara

"NOW, ST. KARL [MARX] COMES FIRST—THE AXIS—AND WILL REMAIN SO FOR HOWEVER MANY YEARS THE SPHEROID HAS ROOM FOR ME ON ITS OUTER MANTLE."

ERNESTO CHE GUEVARA

"REVOLUTIONS, RADICAL AND ACCELERATED
SOCIAL TRANSFORMATIONS, ARE MADE IN
SPECIFIC CIRCUMSTANCES. THEY RARELY,
IF EVER, EMERGE FULLY RIPE, AND NOT ALL
THEIR DETAILS CAN BE SCIENTIFICALLY
FORESEEN. THEY ARE MADE FROM PASSION,
FROM THE IMPROVISATION OF HUMAN BEINGS
IN THEIR STRUGGLE FOR SOCIAL CHANGE,
AND THEY ARE NEVER PERFECT.
OUR REVOLUTION WAS NO EXCEPTION.
IT COMMITTED ERRORS, AND SOME OF
THESE COST US DEARLY."

ERNESTO CHE GUEVARA

CUBA

A REVOLUTION BEGINS
DECEMBER 1956

The history of the military takeover on March 10, 1952—the bloodless coup led by Fulgencio Batista—does not, of course, begin on the day of that barracks revolt. Its antecedents must be sought far back in Cuban history: further back than the intervention of US Ambassador Sumner Welles in 1933; further back still than the Platt Amendment in 1901; much further back than the landing of the hero Narciso López, direct envoy of the US annexationists. We have to go back to John Quincy Adams's times, who, at the beginning of the 19th century, announced his country's policy regarding Cuba: that like an apple torn from Spain, Cuba would fall into the hands of Uncle Sam. These are all links in a long chain of continental aggression that has not been aimed solely at Cuba.

This tide, this ebb and flow of the imperial wave, is marked by the fall of democratic governments and the rise of new ones in the face of uncontainable pressure from the multitudes. History exhibits similar characteristics in all of Latin America: dictatorial governments representing a small minority come to power through coups d'état; democratic governments with a broad popular base arise laboriously and, frequently, even before coming to power, are already compromised by concessions they have had to make beforehand to survive. Although in this sense the Cuban revolution marks an exception in all the Americas, it is necessary to point out the antecedents of this whole process. It was because of this process that the author of these lines, tossed here and there by the waves of social movements convulsing the Americas, had the opportunity to meet another Latin American exile: Fidel Castro.

I met him on one of those cold Mexican nights, and I remember that our first discussion was about international politics. Within a few hours—by dawn—I was one of the future expeditionaries. But I would like to clarify how and why it was in Mexico that I met Cuba's current head of state.

It happened in 1954, during a low-point for democratic governments, when the last Latin American revolutionary democracy still standing—that of Jacobo Árbenz—succumbed to cold, premeditated aggression, conducted by the United States behind the smokescreen of its continental propaganda. The visible head of that aggression was US Secretary of State John Foster Dulles, who by a strange coincidence was also the lawyer for and a stockholder in the United Fruit Company, the main imperialist enterprise in Guatemala.

I had departed from Guatemala defeated, united with all Guatemalans by the pain, hoping, searching for a way to rebuild that anguished country's future.

And Fidel came to Mexico looking for neutral ground in which to prepare his forces for the big effort. An internal split had already occurred after the assault on the Moncada military garrison in Santiago de Cuba. All the weak at heart had split away, those who for one reason or another joined political parties or revolutionary groups which demanded less sacrifice. New recruits were already joining the freshly formed ranks of what was called the July 26 Movement, named after the date of the 1953 attack on the Moncada garrison. For those in charge of training these people – under necessarily clandestine conditions in Mexico – an extremely difficult task was beginning. They were fighting against the Mexican government, agents of the FBI, and also those of Batista – three forces that in one way or another joined together, for whom money and buying people off were essential tools. In addition, we had to struggle against [Rafael] Trujillo's spies and against the poor selection of the human material – especially in Miami. And after overcoming all these difficulties we had to accomplish something extremely important: we had to depart... and then... arrive [in Cuba], and all the rest, which, at the time, seemed easy to us. Today we can measure how much it all cost in effort, sacrifice, and lives.

Aided by a small, intimate team, Fidel Castro gave himself, all his energy, and his extraordinary work spirit entirely to the task of organizing the armed combatants who were to leave for Cuba. He almost never gave classes on military tactics, since time for him was in short supply. The rest of us were able to learn quite a bit from Commander Alberto Bayo [a veteran of the Spanish Civil War]. Listening to those first classes, my almost immediate impression was that victory was, in fact, possible. It had seemed doubtful when I first enrolled with the rebel commander, to whom I was attached from the beginning by a leaning toward romantic adventure and the notion that it would be well worth dying on a foreign beach for such pure ideals.

Several months passed in this way. Our marksmanship began to improve, and the best shooters emerged. We found a ranch in Mexico where – under Commander Bayo's direction and with myself as head of personnel – the final preparations were made, aiming to leave in March 1956. Around that time, however, two Mexican police units—both on Batista's payroll—were hunting Fidel Castro, and one of them had the good fortune, in financial terms, to capture him; but they made the absurd error, also financial, of not killing him after taking him prisoner. Within a few days many of his followers were captured. Our ranch on the outskirts of Mexico City also fell into police hands, and we all went to jail.

This all postponed the beginning of the last part of the first stage.

Some of us were imprisoned for 57 days, which we counted off one by one, with the perennial threat of extradition hanging over our heads (as Commander Calixto García and I can attest). But at no time did we lose our personal confidence in Fidel Castro. And Fidel did some things we could almost say compromised his revolutionary discipline for the sake of friendship. I remember explaining my specific case to him: a foreigner, in Mexico illegally, with a whole series of charges against me. I told him that by no means should the revolution be held up on my account; that he could leave me behind; that I understood the situation and would try to fight wherever I was sent; and that the only effort on my behalf should be to have me sent to a nearby country and not to Argentina. I also remember Fidel's sharp reply: "I will not abandon you." And he didn't, and precious time and money had to be diverted to get us out of the Mexican jail. Fidel's personal commitment toward people he holds in esteem is the key to the fanatical loyalty he inspires. Adherence to principles and adherence to the individual combine to make the Rebel Army an indivisible fist.

The days passed as we worked clandestinely, hiding ourselves where we could, shunning public appearances to the extent possible, hardly going out into the streets. After several months, we discovered there was a traitor in our ranks, whose name we did not know and who had sold a shipment of arms. We also learned that he had sold the yacht and a transmitter, although he had not yet drawn up the "legal contract" of the sale. That first instalment served to show the Cuban authorities that the traitor, in fact, knew our internal workings; but it also saved us, since it showed us the same thing.

From that moment on, our preparations were necessarily feverish. The *Granma* was put into shape at an extraordinary speed. We piled up as many provisions as we could get — very few, in fact — along with uniforms, rifles, equipment, and two anti-tank guns with hardly any ammunition. Finally, on November 25, 1956, at 2:00 a.m., we set out to make Fidel's words — mocked by the official press — real: "In 1956 we will be free or we will be martyrs."

We left the port of Tuxpan with our lights out, an infernal heap of men and all types of equipment. We had very bad weather, yet although sea travel was prohibited, the estuary remained calm. We entered the Gulf of Mexico and shortly after turned on the lights. We made a frantic search for antihistamines to combat seasickness, and could not find them. We sang the Cuban national anthem and the July 26 hymn for a total of perhaps five minutes, and then the whole boat assumed a ridiculous, tragic appearance: men clutching their stomachs, anguish written in their faces, some with their heads in buckets, others lying immobile on the deck in strange positions, their clothes covered in vomit. With the exception of two or three sailors, and four or five others, the rest of the 82 crew members were seasick. But after the fourth or fifth day, the general panorama improved slightly. We discovered that what we thought was a leak in the boat was actually an open plumbing faucet. We had already thrown anything superfluous overboard in order to lighten the ballast.

The route we had chosen involved making a wide turn south

of Cuba, bordering Jamaica and the Grand Cayman Islands, and landing someplace close to the village of Niquero in Oriente province. We were progressing quite slowly. On November 30 we heard over the radio news of the uprising in Santiago de Cuba, started by our great Frank País, to coincide with the expedition's arrival. The following day, December 1, at night, we set the bow on a straight line toward Cuba, desperately seeking the Cape Cruz lighthouse as we ran out of water, food, and fuel.

At 2 a.m., on a black, stormy night, the situation was disturbing. The lookouts paced back and forth, searching for the ray of light that refused to appear on the horizon. [Roberto] Roque, an ex-navy lieutenant, once again climbed on to the small upper bridge, looking for light from the cape. Losing his footing, he fell into the water. Shortly after continuing on our way, we saw the light; but the labored advance of our boat made the final hours of the trip interminable. It was already daylight when we reached Cuba at a place known as Belic on Las Coloradas beach.

A coastguard boat spotted us and radioed the discovery to Batista's army. We had just disembarked and entered the swamp, in great haste and carrying only vital supplies, when enemy planes attacked us. Walking through the mangroves, we naturally could not be seen or pursued by the planes, but the dictatorship's army was already on our trail. It took us several hours to get out of the swamp, where we had ended up due to the inexperience and irresponsibility of a compañero who said he knew the way. We wound up on solid ground, lost, walking in circles.

We were an army of shadows, ghosts, walking as if to the beat of some dark, psychic mechanism. The crossing had been seven days of constant hunger and seasickness, followed by three more days — terrible days — on land. Exactly 10 days after the departure from Mexico, in the early hours of December 5, after a night march interrupted by fainting, exhaustion, and rest for the troops, we reached a point known—paradoxically—by the name of Alegría de Pío [joy of the pious]. It was a small grove of trees, bordering a sugarcane field on one side and open to some valleys on the other, with dense woods starting farther back. The place was ill-suited for camp, but we stopped anyway to rest for a day and resume our march the following night.

From: *Reminiscences of the Cuban Revolutionary War* by Ernesto Che Guevara

ALEGRÍA DE PÍO
DECEMBER 1956

Alegría de Pío is in Oriente province, Niquero municipality, near Cape Cruz, where on December 5, 1956, the dictatorship's forces caught us unawares.

We were exhausted from a trek that was not so much long as painful. We had landed on December 2, at a place known as Las Coloradas beach. We had lost almost all our equipment, and wearing new boots had trudged endlessly through saltwater swamps. Almost the entire troop was suffering open blisters on their feet; but boots and fungal infections were not our only enemies. We reached Cuba following a seven-day voyage across the Gulf of Mexico and the Caribbean Sea, without food, in a poorly maintained boat, almost everyone plagued by seasickness from not being used to sea travel. We left the port of Tuxpan on November 25, a day with a stiff wind when all sea travel was prohibited. All this had left its mark on our troop made up of raw recruits who had never seen combat.

All we had left of our equipment for war was nothing but our rifles, cartridge belts, and a few wet rounds of ammunition. Our medical supplies had vanished, and most of our backpacks had been left behind in the swamps. The previous night we had passed through one of the cane fields of the Niquero sugar mill, owned at the time by Julio Lobo. We had managed to satisfy our hunger and thirst by eating sugarcane, but lacking experience we had left a trail of cane peelings and bagasse. Not that the guards following our steps needed any trail, for it had been our guide—as we found out years later—who betrayed us and brought them to us. When we stopped to rest the night before, we let him go—an error we were to repeat several times during our long struggle until we learned that civilians whose backgrounds we did not know could not be trusted in dangerous areas. In the circumstances, we should never have permitted that false guide to leave.

By daybreak on December 5 only a few could take another step. On the verge of collapse, we would walk a short distance and then beg for a long rest. Thus debilitated, orders were given to halt on the edge of a cane field, in some bushes close to dense woods. Most of us slept through the morning hours.

At noon we noticed unusual activity. Piper planes as well as other small army and private aircraft began to circle. Some of our group continued peacefully cutting and eating sugarcane, not realizing they were perfectly visible to those flying the enemy planes, which were now circling at slow speed and low altitude. I was the troop physician and it was my duty to treat everyone's blistered feet. I recall my last patient that morning: his name was compañero Humberto Lamotte and it was to be his last day on earth. In my mind's eye I see how tired and anguished he was as he walked from my improvised first-aid station to his post, carrying in one hand the shoes he could not wear.

Compañero [Jesús] Montané and I were leaning against a tree talking about our respective children, eating our meager rations— half a sausage and two crackers—when we heard a shot. Within seconds, a hail of bullets—at least that's how it seemed to us, this being our baptism of fire—descended on our group of 82 men. My rifle was not one of the best; I had deliberately asked for it because

I was in terrible physical condition due to a prolonged asthma attack I had endured throughout our whole maritime voyage, and I did not want to be held responsible for wasting a good weapon. I can hardly remember what followed; my memory is already hazy. After the initial burst of gunfire, [Juan] Almeida, then a captain, approached requesting orders, but there was no one to issue them. Later I was told that Fidel had tried in vain to gather everybody into the adjoining cane field, which could be reached just by crossing a boundary path. The surprise had been too great and the gunfire too heavy. Almeida ran back to take charge of his group. A compañero dropped a box of ammunition at my feet. I pointed to it, and he answered me with an anguished expression, which I remember perfectly, and which seemed to say, "It's too late for ammunition." He immediately took the path to the cane field. (He was later murdered by Batista's henchmen.)

This might have been the first time I was faced, literally, with the dilemma of choosing between my devotion to medicine and my duty as a revolutionary soldier. There, at my feet, was a back-pack full of medicine and a box of ammunition. They were too heavy to carry both. I picked up the ammunition, leaving the medicine, and started to cross the clearing, heading for the cane field. I remember Faustino Pérez, on his knees in the bushes, firing his submachine gun. Near me, a compañero named [Emilio] Albentosa was walking toward the cane field. A burst of gunfire hit us both. I felt a sharp blow to my chest and a wound in my neck; I thought for certain I was dead. Albentosa, vomiting blood and bleeding profusely from a deep wound made by a .45-caliber bullet, screamed something like, "They've killed me," and began to fire his rifle although there was no one there. Flat on the ground, I said to Faustino, "I'm fucked," and Faustino, still shooting, looked at me and told me it was nothing, but I saw in his eyes he considered me as good as dead.

Still on the ground, I fired a shot toward the woods, on an impulse like that of my wounded companion. I immediately began to think about the best way to die, since in that minute all seemed lost. I remembered an old Jack London story in which the hero, aware that he is about to freeze to death in Alaskan ice, leans against a tree and prepares to die with dignity. That was the only thing that came to my mind. Someone, on his knees, shouted that we should surrender, and I heard a voice — later I found out it belonged to Camilo Cienfuegos — shouting, "No one surrenders here!" followed by a swear word. [José] Ponce approached me, agitated and breathing hard. He showed me a bullet wound that appeared to have pierced his lungs. He told me he was wounded and I replied, indifferently, that I was as well. Then Ponce, along with other unhurt compañeros, crawled toward the cane field. For a moment I was alone, just lying there waiting to die. Almeida approached, urging me to go on, and despite the intense pain I dragged myself into the cane field. There I saw the great compañero Raúl Suárez, whose thumb had been blown away by a bullet, being attended by Faustino Pérez, who was bandaging his hand. Then everything blurred — low-flying airplanes strafing the field, adding to the confusion — amid scenes that were at once Dantesque and grotesque, such as an overweight combatant trying to hide behind a single sugarcane stalk, or a man who kept yelling for silence in the din of gunfire, for no apparent reason.

A group was organized, headed by Almeida, including Commander Ramiro Valdés, in that period a lieutenant, and compañeros [Rafael] Chao and [Reynaldo] Benítez. With Almeida leading, we crossed the last path among the rows of sugarcane and reached the safety of the woods. The first shouts of "Fire!" were heard from the cane field and columns of flame and smoke began to rise. But I can't be sure about that. I was thinking more of the bitterness of defeat and the imminence of my death.

We walked until darkness made it impossible to go on, and decided to lie down and go to sleep huddled together in a heap. We were starving and thirsty, the mosquitoes adding to our misery. This was our baptism of fire, December 5, 1956, on the outskirts of Niquero. Such was the beginning of forging what would become the Rebel Army.

From: *Reminiscences of the Cuban Revolutionary War* by Ernesto Che Guevara

A FAMOUS INTERVIEW
APRIL 1957

In mid-April 1957 we returned with our mountain army-in training to the region of Palma Mocha, near Turquino Peak. During that period our most valuable men for fighting in the mountains were those of peasant stock.

Guillermo García and Ciro Frías, with patrols of peasants, came and went from place to place in the Sierra Maestra, bringing news, scouting, getting food; in a word, they were the mobile forward guard of our column. We were once again in the region of Arroyo del Infierno, the site of one of our battles, and peasants who came to greet us described the tragic details of that attack: exactly who had led the soldiers directly to our camp and who had died. In fact, the peasants, well versed in the art of the gossip, amply informed us about life in the region.

Fidel, who had no radio in those days, asked to borrow one from a local peasant, who agreed, and so via a large radio carried in a combatant's backpack we were able to hear the news direct from Havana. There was a brief period of freedom of speech due to the reestablishment of the so-called [civil] guarantees.

Guillermo García, brilliantly disguised as a Batista army corporal, and two compañeros disguised as army soldiers, went to look for the informer who had led the army to us. They brought him back the following day "on the colonel's order." The man had been tricked, but when he saw the ragged army he knew what awaited him. With great cynicism he told us everything about his relations with the army and how he had told "that bastard Casillas" that he would be perfectly willing to take the army to where we were and capture us, for he had spied on us; they had not, however, listened to him.

On one of those days, in one of those hills, the informer was executed and his remains buried on a ridge of the Sierra Maestra. We received a message from Celia announcing she was coming with two North American journalists who wanted to interview Fidel, under the pretext of seeing the three little gringos. She also sent some money collected from sympathizers of the movement.

It was decided that Lalo Sardiñas would bring the North Americans in through the region of Estrada Palma, which he knew well as a former merchant in the region. We were dedicating our time to making contact with peasants who could serve as links and who could maintain permanent camps to use as contact centers for the whole region, which was growing in size. We located houses to use as supply centers for our troops, and set up warehouses from which we drew supplies as we needed them. These places also served as rest stops for the fast human stagecoaches that moved along the edge of the Sierra Maestra carrying messages and news.

These messengers had an extraordinary ability to cover very long distances in very little time, and we constantly found ourselves fooled by their version of "a half-hour's walk" or "just over there." For the peasants this was almost always spot on, even though their concept of time and the length of an hour had little to do with that of a city dweller.

Three days after the order was given to Lalo Sardiñas, we heard news that six people were coming up through the region of Santo Domingo: two women, two gringos — the journalists — and two others no one knew. We also received some contradictory news, however, to the effect that the Rural Guard had discovered their presence through an informer, and had surrounded a house they were staying in.

News travels with extraordinary speed in the Sierra Maestra, but it is also distorted. Camilo went out with a platoon, with the order to free the North Americans and Celia Sánchez at all costs; we knew Celia was coming with the group. They arrived, however, safe and sound. The false alarm was due to enemy troop movements prompted by an informer; in those days informers were easy to find among backward peasants.

On April 23, the journalist Bob Taber and a photographer arrived at our camp. With them came compañeras Celia Sánchez and Haydée Santamaría and the men sent by the movement in the *Llano* [urban underground, literally "plains"]: Marcos or "Nicaragua" — Commander [Carlos] Iglesias — today governor of Las Villas and in those days in charge of armed actions in Santiago; and Marcelo Fernández, who was coordinator of the movement and today is president of the National Bank. As he knew English, he acted as interpreter.

The days went according to schedule; we tried to demonstrate our strength to the North Americans and evade their more indiscreet questions. We knew nothing about these journalists; still, they interviewed the three boys who answered their questions very well, demonstrating the new spirit they had developed in the primitive life among us, despite their difficulty in adjusting and the fact that we had little in common.

We were also joined by one of the dearest and most likable figures of our revolutionary war, Vaquerito [Roberto Rodríguez]. Together with another compañero, Vaquerito found us one day saying he had spent over a month looking for us, and that he was from Morón in Camagüey. As always in such cases, we interrogated him, and then gave him the rudiments of a political orientation, a task that frequently fell to me. Vaquerito did not have a political idea in his head, and did not seem to be anything other than a happy and healthy young man, who saw all of this as a marvelous adventure. He came barefoot and Celia lent him an extra pair of her shoes, which were leather and the kind worn in Mexico. Owing to his small stature, they were the only shoes that fit him. With the new shoes and a large straw hat, he looked like a Mexican cowboy or *vaquero*, and that is how the nickname Vaquerito was born.

As is well known, Vaquerito did not see the end of the revolutionary struggle, for as head of the "suicide squad" of Column 8, he died one day before Santa Clara was taken. Of his life among us, we all remember his extraordinary gaity, his perpetual cheerfulness, and the strange and novel way he confronted danger. Vaquerito was an amazing liar; perhaps he never had a conversation in which he did not adorn the truth so much that it was practically unrecognizable. But as a messenger, which he was in the early days, and later as a combatant and as head of the "suicide squad," Vaquerito demonstrated that for him, there was no precise border between reality and fantasy, and the same feats his agile mind invented he was able to carry out on the battlefield. His extreme bravery became legendary by the time our epic war was over, which he did not live to see.

It occurred to me once, after one of our nightly reading sessions sometime after he had joined us, to question Vaquerito. He began to tell us about his life, and we began surreptitiously calculating his age, pencils in hand. When he finished, after many witty anecdotes, we asked him how old he was. Vaquerito was a little over 20, but adding up all of his deeds and jobs, it seemed that he had started working five years before he was born.

Compañero Nicaragua brought news of more weapons in Santiago—what was left from the assault on the presidential palace. He reported there were 10 automatic rifles, 11 Johnson rifles, and six short carbines. There were a few more, but plans were under way to open another front in the region of the Miranda sugar mill. Fidel opposed this idea and only allowed a few arms for the second front, giving orders that all possible weapons be brought up to reinforce ours. We continued marching, putting a distance between ourselves and the uncomfortable company of some guards who were marauding nearby. But first we decided to climb Turquino. The ascent of our highest mountain had an almost mystical significance for us, and anyway, we were already quite close to the peak.

The entire column climbed Turquino Peak and up there we finished the interview with Bob Taber. He was preparing a film that was later shown in the United States, at a time when we were not feared so much. (One illustrative note: a peasant who joined us told us that Casillas had offered him 300 pesos and a pregnant cow if he killed Fidel. The North Americans were not the only ones wrong about the price of our highest commander.)

According to our altimeter, Turquino Peak was 1,850 meters above sea level. I note this as an incidental point — for we never properly tested the instrument — but at sea level it worked well and this figure differs substantially from that given in official records.

Since the army was on our heels, Guillermo was sent with a group of compañeros as snipers. Thanks to my asthma I had no extra strength, and was obliged to walk at the end of the column; I was also relieved of the Thompson submachine gun I was carrying. About three days passed before I got it back, which were some of the most bitter days in the Sierra Maestra for me, for I was unarmed while every day there was the possibility of encounters with the enemy.

In May 1957, two of the North American boys left the column with the journalist Bob Taber, who had finished his story, and they reached Guantánamo safe and sound. We continued to march slowly along the ridge of the Sierra Maestra and its slopes. We were making contacts, exploring new regions, and spreading the revolutionary flame and the legend of our *barbudos* across the Sierra Maestra. The new spirit was communicated far and wide. Peasants came to greet us without so much fear, and we also feared them less. Our relative strength had increased considerably and we felt more secure against any surprise attack by Batista's army, and closer friends with our peasants.

From: *Reminiscences of the Cuban Revolutionary War* by Ernesto Che Guevara

ON THE MARCH
MAY 1957

The two weeks of May [1957] were a continual march toward our objective. At the beginning of the month, we were on a hill near the ridge close to Turquino Peak. We were crossing regions that later became theaters of many revolutionary victories. We passed through Santa Ana and El Hombrito; later on, at Pico Verde, we found Escudero's house, and continued until we reached the Loma del Burro. We were moving eastward, looking for weapons that were supposed to be sent from Santiago and hidden in the region of the Loma del Burro, close to Oro de Guisa. One night on this journey that lasted a couple of weeks, while going to carry out a trivial mission, I confused the paths and was lost for two days until I found everyone again in El Hombrito. I was then able to see for myself that we each carried on our backs everything necessary for individual survival: salt and oil—very important—canned food and milk, everything required for sleeping, making fire, and cooking, and the instrument I had relied on very heavily until then, a compass.

Finding myself lost, the next morning I took out the compass and, guiding myself by it, continued for a day and a half until realizing I was becoming even more lost. I approached a peasant hut and the people directed me to the rebel camp. Later we found that in such rugged territory a compass can only provide a general orientation, never a definite course; either one has to be led by guides or to know the terrain oneself, as we came to know it when later operating in that same region.

I was very moved by the warm reception that greeted me when I rejoined the column. When I arrived they had just completed a people's trial in which three informers had been tried and judged; one of them, Nápoles, was condemned to death. Camilo was the president of that trial.

In that period I was still working as a doctor and in each little village or hamlet I set up a consultation area. It was monotonous, for I had little medicine to offer and the clinical cases in the Sierra Maestra were all more or less the same: prematurely aged and toothless women, children with distended bellies, parasites, rickets, general vitamin deficiencies — these were the stains of the Sierra Maestra. Even today they continue, but to a much lesser degree. The children of those mothers of the Sierra Maestra have gone to study at the Camilo Cienfuegos School City, they are growing up healthy, different kids from those first undernourished inhabitants of our pioneer school city.

I remember one girl was watching the consultations I was giving to the local women, who came in with an almost religious attitude toward finding the sources of their sufferings. When her mother arrived, the little girl — after attentively watching several previous examinations in the hut that served as a clinic — gaily remarked, "Mamá, this doctor says the same thing to everyone!"

And it was absolutely true; my knowledge was good for little else. They all had the same clinical symptoms, and without knowing it they each told the same heartbreaking story. What would have happened if the doctor had diagnosed the strange exhaustion suffered by the young mother of several children, when she carried buckets of water from the river to the house, as being simply due to too much work on such a meager diet? Her exhaustion is inexplicable to her, since all her life she had carried the same buckets of water to the same place and only now does she feel tired. The people in the Sierra Maestra grow like wild flowers, untended and without care, and they wear themselves out rapidly, working without reward. We began to feel in our bones the need for a definitive change in the lives of these people. The idea of agrarian reform became clear, and communion with the people ceased being theory and became a fundamental part of our being.

The guerrilla group and the peasantry began to merge into one single mass, although no one could say at what point on the long road this happened, or at what moment words became reality and we became a part of the peasant masses. I only know that for me, those consultations with the peasants of the Sierra Maestra converted my spontaneous and somewhat lyrical resolve into a different, more serene force. Those suffering and loyal inhabitants of the Sierra Maestra have never suspected the role they played in forging our revolutionary ideology...

From: *Reminiscences of the Cuban Revolutionary War* by Ernesto Che Guevara

CARING FOR THE WOUNDED
MAY–JUNE 1957

...On the banks of the Peladero River lived the overseer of a large land estate, David [Gómez] was his name, and he cooperated greatly with us. Once David killed a cow for us and we simply had to go out and get it. The animal had been slaughtered on the riverbank and cut into pieces; we had to move the meat by night. I sent the first group with Israel Pardo in front, and then the second led by Banderas. Banderas was quite undisciplined and did not follow orders. He let the others carry the full weight of the carcass, and it took all night to move it. A small troop was now being formed under my command, since Almeida was wounded. Conscious of my responsibility, I notified Banderas that unless he changed his attitude he was no longer a combatant, but merely a sympathizer. He really did change then; he was never the model of a combatant when it came to discipline, but he was one of those enterprising and broad-minded men, simple and ingenuous, whose eyes were opened to reality through the shock of the revolution. He had been cultivating his small, isolated parcel of land in the woods, and he had a true passion for trees and agriculture. He lived in a small shack with two little pigs, each with its name, and a little dog. One day he showed me a portrait of his two sons who lived with his ex-wife in Santiago. He explained to me that some day, when the revolution triumphed, he would be able to go some place where he could really grow something, not like this inhospitable piece of land virtually hanging from the mountaintop.

I spoke to him of cooperatives, although he did not understand my point very well. He wanted to work the land on his own, by his own efforts; nevertheless, little by little I managed to convince him that it was better to work with others, and that machinery would increase his productivity. Banderas would today have undoubtedly been a vanguard fighter in the area of agricultural production. In the Sierra Maestra he taught himself to read and write and was preparing for the future. He was an enlightened peasant who knew the value of contributing through his own efforts to writing a page of history.

I had a long conversation with the overseer David, who asked me for a list of all the important things we needed; he was going to Santiago and would pick them up there. He was a typical overseer, loyal to his boss, contemptuous of the peasants, racist. When the army, however, learned of his relations with us and took him prisoner and tortured him barbarously, his first concern on returning was to convince us — we had thought him dead — that he did not talk. I do not know if David is in Cuba today, or if he followed his old bosses whose land was confiscated by the revolution. Although he was a man who felt the need for a change, who understood how urgent change was, he never imagined that it would also reach him and his world. The revolution has been built on the sincere efforts of many ordinary people. Our mission is to develop what is good and noble in each person, to convert every person into a revolutionary, from the Davids who did not understand very well, to the Banderases, who died without seeing the dawn. Blind and unrewarded sacrifices also made the revolution. Those of us who today see its achievements have the responsibility to remember those who fell along the way, and to work for a future where there will be fewer stragglers.

From: *Reminiscences of the Cuban Revolutionary War* by Ernesto Che Guevara

ON BECOMING A COMMANDER
JULY 1957

...The Sierra Manifesto, dated July 12, 1957, was published in the newspapers of the time. For us, this declaration was nothing more than a brief pause on the road. Our fundamental task—to defeat the oppressor's army on the battlefield—remained. A new column was being organized then, with myself in charge, and I became a captain. There were other promotions: Ramiro Valdés became a captain and his platoon joined my column. Ciro Redondo was also promoted to captain, and was to lead a platoon. The column was made up of three platoons. The first, led by Lalo Sardiñas, made up the forward guard, and he was also second-in-command. Ramiro Valdés and Ciro Redondo led the other two platoons. Our column, [Column 4] named the "Dispossessed Peasants," was made up of close to 75 combatants, variously dressed and armed; nonetheless, I was very proud of them. Some nights later, I felt even prouder, and even closer to the revolution, if that were possible, even more anxious to prove my military award was well deserved...

We sent a letter of congratulations and appreciation to "Carlos," Frank País's underground name, who was living his final days. It was signed by all the officers of the guerrilla army who knew how to write (many of the Sierra Maestra peasants were not very skilled in this art but were already an important component of the guerrillas). The signatures appeared in two columns, and as we wrote down the ranks in the second one, when my turn came, Fidel simply said, "Make it commander." In this most informal way, almost in passing, I became commander of the second column of the guerrilla army, which would later become known as Column 4.

The letter, written in a peasant's house — although I don't remember where — was the guerrilla fighters' warm message to their brother in the city, fighting so heroically in Santiago to obtain supplies for us and alleviate the enemy's pressure.

There is a bit of vanity hiding within every one of us, and I felt like the proudest man in the world that day. The symbol of my promotion, a small star, was given to me by Celia, and came with a gift: one of the wristwatches ordered from Manzanillo. With my recently formed column, my first task was to set a trap for Sánchez Mosquera, but he was the most devious all of Batista's henchmen and had already left the area.

We had to do something to justify the semi-independent life we were to lead in what was to be our new zone, the region of El Hombrito where we were headed, so we began to plan a series of great deeds.

We had to prepare to celebrate with dignity the approaching glorious date of July 26, and Fidel gave me free rein to do whatever I could, with prudence. At the last meeting we met a new doctor who had joined the guerrilla forces: Sergio del Valle, now chief of the general staff of our revolutionary army. At that time he practiced his profession as far as the conditions of the Sierra Maestra allowed...

From: *Reminiscences of the Cuban Revolutionary War* by Ernesto Che Guevara

THE MURDERED PUPPY
NOVEMBER 1957

For all the harshness of conditions in the Sierra Maestra, the day was superb. We were hiking through Agua Revés, one of the steepest and most labyrinthine valleys in the Turquino basin, patiently following Sánchez Mosquera's troops. The relentless killer had left a trail of burned-out farms, sadness, and despair throughout the entire region. But his trail led him, by necessity, to ascend along one of the two or three points of the Sierra Maestra where we knew Camilo would be: either the Nevada ridge, or the area we called the "ridge of the crippled," now known as the "ridge of the dead."

Camilo had left hurriedly with about a dozen combatants, part of his forward guard; this small number had to be divided up in three different places to stop a column of over 100 soldiers. My mission was to attack Sánchez Mosquera from behind and surround him. Our fundamental aim was encirclement; we therefore followed him patiently, over a considerable distance, past the painful trail of burning peasant houses, set alight by the enemy's rear guard. The enemy troops were far away, but we could hear their shouts. We didn't know how many there were in all. Our column advanced with difficulty along the slopes, while the enemy advanced through the center of a narrow valley.

Everything would have been perfect had it not been for our new mascot, a little hunting dog only a few weeks old. Despite repeated attempts by Félix [Mendoza] to scare the animal back to our center of operations — a house where the cooks were staying — the puppy continued to follow behind the column. In that part of the Sierra Maestra it is extremely difficult to move along the slopes because there are no trails. We made it through a difficult spot where the "tomb" — old, dead trees — was covered by new growth, although the going was extremely laborious. We jumped over the tree trunks and bushes trying not to lose contact with our guides.

In these conditions the small column marched in silence, hardly a broken branch disturbing the usual murmurings of the mountain. But suddenly, this code of silence was broken by the disconsolate, nervous barking of the pup. He was falling behind and was desperately barking for his owners to come and get him out of his trouble. Somebody went and picked up the little animal and we continued, but as we were resting in a creek bed with a lookout keeping an eye on enemy movements, the dog started up again with its hysterical howling. Comforting words no longer had any effect; the animal, afraid we would leave it behind, howled desperately.

I remember my emphatic order, "Félix, that dog must stop its howling once and for all. You're in charge; strangle it. There will be no more barking." Félix regarded me with eyes that said nothing. In the middle of our exhausted ranks, as if marking the center of a circle, stood Félix and the dog. Very slowly he took out a rope, placed it around the animal's neck, and began to pull. The affectionate movements of the dog's tail suddenly became convulsive, before gradually dying out, accompanied by a steady moan that escaped from its throat, despite the firm grip. I don't know how long it took for the end to come, but to all of us it seemed like forever. The puppy, after a last nervous shudder, stopped writhing. There it lay, sprawled out, its little head spread over the twigs.

We continued the march without a word said about the incident. Sánchez Mosquera's troops had gained some ground and shortly afterward we heard gunfire. We quickly descended the slopes, amid the difficult terrain, searching for the best path to reach the rear guard. We knew that Camilo had attacked. It took us a considerable amount of time to reach the last house before starting up the other side, moving carefully because we imagined that we might come upon the enemy any moment. The exchange of fire had been intense, but it had not lasted long and we were all tense with expectation. The last house was abandoned. There was no sign of the troops. Two scouts climbed the "ridge of the crippled" and soon returned with the news: "There is a grave up above. We dug it up and found one of the metal-heads [soldiers] buried." They also brought the identity papers of the victim, found in his shirt pocket. There had been a clash and one man was killed. The dead man was theirs, but that was all we knew.

We returned slowly, discouraged. Two scouting parties came upon a large number of footprints along both sides of the ridge of the Sierra Maestra, but nothing else. We made the return trip slowly, this time through the valley.

We arrived during the night at a house, also vacant. It was the Mar Verde homestead where we could rest. Soon, a pig was cooked along with some yucca, and we ate. Someone started to sing along to a guitar, since the peasant's houses had been hastily abandoned with all their belongings still inside.

I don't know whether it was the sentimental tune, or the darkness of night, or just plain exhaustion. What happened is that Félix—seated on the ground to eat—dropped a bone. One of the house dogs came up meekly and took it. Félix put his hand on its head, and the dog looked at him. Félix looked back at the dog, and then he and I exchanged a guilty look. We suddenly fell silent.

An imperceptible stirring came over us. There, in our presence, with its mild, mischievous and slightly reproachful gaze, observing us through the eyes of another dog, was the murdered puppy.

From: *Reminiscences of the Cuban Revolutionary War* by Ernesto Che Guevara

ONE YEAR OF ARMED STRUGGLE
DECEMBER 1957

By the beginning of 1958 we had completed more than a year of struggle. A brief account of our military, organizational, and political situation at that point is necessary, as is a description of how we were progressing.

Regarding our military situation, let us briefly recall that our troop had disembarked on December 2, 1956, at Las Coloradas beach. Three days later, on December 5, we were surprised and beaten at Alegría de Pío. By the end of the month, we had regrouped to begin small-scale actions, appropriate to our strength, at La Plata, a small barracks on the banks of the river of the same name, on the southern coast of Oriente.

The fundamental characteristic of our troop, during the whole period between disembarking, the immediate defeat at Alegría de Pío, and the battle of El Uvero was that it was one single guerrilla group, led by Fidel Castro, and constantly mobile (we could call this the nomadic phase).

Between December 2, [1956], and May 28, [1957], the date of the battle of El Uvero, we slowly established links with the city. During this period, these relations were characterized by lack of understanding on the part of the urban leadership [of the July 26 Movement] of our importance as the vanguard of the revolution and of Fidel's stature as its leader.

Then, two distinct opinions began to crystallize regarding tactics to be followed. They corresponded to two distinct concepts of strategy, which were thereafter known as the *Sierra* [guerrilla movement] and the *Llano* [urban underground]. Our discussions and our internal conflicts were quite sharp. Nevertheless, the fundamental concerns of this phase were survival and the establishment of a guerrilla base.

The reactions of the peasants have already been analyzed many times. Immediately after the Alegría de Pío disaster, we felt their warm camaraderie and spontaneous support for our defeated troop. After the regrouping and the first clashes, and the simultaneous repression by Batista's army, terror spread among the peasants and a coldness toward our forces appeared. The fundamental problem was that if they saw us, they had to denounce us. If the army learned of our presence through other sources, they were lost. Denouncing us went against their conscience and, in any case, put them in danger, since revolutionary justice was swift.

In spite of a terrorized, or at least neutralized and insecure peasantry, which chose to avoid this serious dilemma by leaving the Sierra Maestra, our army was increasingly entrenching itself. We were taking possession of the terrain and achieving absolute control of a zone of the Sierra Maestra extending beyond Turquino Peak in the east and toward Caracas Peak in the west. Little by little, as the peasants saw the length of the struggle and that the guerrillas were invincible, they began to respond more rationally, joining our army as combatants. From then on, they not only filled our ranks, they also grouped themselves around us and the guerrilla army became strongly entrenched in the countryside, especially since the peasants usually had relatives throughout the entire zone. We called this "dressing the guerrillas in palm leaves."

The column was strengthened not only through the support of the peasants and individual volunteers, but also by forces sent from the national committee [of the July 26 Movement] and the Oriente provincial committee, which had considerable autonomy. In the period between the disembarkation and El Uvero, a column arrived consisting of some 50 men divided into five combat platoons, each with a weapon, although these were all different and only 30 were good quality. The battles of La Plata and Arroyo del Infierno took place before this group joined us. We had been taken by surprise in Altos de Espinosa, losing one of our men there; the same thing almost happened in the Gaviro region, after a traitor, whose mission was to kill Fidel, led the army to us three times.

The bitter experiences of these surprises and our arduous life in the mountains were tempering us as veterans. The new troop received its baptism of fire in the battle of El Uvero. This action was of great importance because it marked the point at which we carried out a frontal attack in broad daylight against a well-defended post. It was one of the bloodiest episodes of the war, taking into account the length of the battle and the number of participants. As a consequence of this clash, the enemy was dislodged from the coastal zones of the Sierra Maestra.

After El Uvero, our smaller column — of the wounded under my care and other individual combatants who had joined us — rejoined the principal column. I was named chief of the second column, called Column 4, which operated east of Turquino. It is worth noting that the column led personally by Fidel operated primarily to the west of Turquino Peak, and ours on the other side, as far as we could extend ourselves. There was a certain tactical independence of command, but we were under Fidel's orders and kept in touch with him every week or two by messenger.

The division of forces coincided with the July 26 anniversary, and while the troops of [Fidel's] "José Martí" Column 1 attacked Estrada Palma in a series of actions, we marched rapidly toward the settlement of Bueycito, which we attacked and took in our column's first battle. Between that time and the first days of January 1958, the consolidation of rebel territory was achieved. In order to penetrate this territory, the army had to concentrate its forces and advance in strong columns; their preparations were extensive and results limited, since they lacked mobility. Various enemy columns were encircled and others decimated, or at least halted. Our knowledge of the area and our maneuverability increased, and we entered a sedentary period, one of fixed encampments. In the first attack on Pino del Agua we used subtler methods, fooling the enemy completely, since by then we were familiar with their habits, which were as Fidel anticipated: a few days after he let himself be seen in the area, the punitive expedition would arrive… my troops would ambush it, and meanwhile, Fidel would pop up elsewhere.

At the end of the year, the enemy troops retreated once more from the Sierra Maestra, and we remained in control of the territory between Caracas Peak and Pino del Agua, on the west and east. To the south was the sea, and the army occupied the small villages on the slopes of the Sierra Maestra to the north.

Our area of operations was broadly extended when Pino del Agua was attacked for the second time by our entire troop under the personal command of Fidel. Two new columns were formed, the "Frank País" Column 6, commanded by Raúl, and Almeida's column. Both had come out of Column 1, commanded by Fidel, which was a steady source of these offshoots, created to establish our forces in distant territories.

This was a period of consolidation for our army, lasting until the second battle of Pino del Agua on February 16, 1958. It was characterized by deadlock: we had insufficient forces to attack the enemy's fortified and relatively easily defended positions, while they did not advance on us.

In our camp, we had suffered the deaths of the *Granma* martyrs, each of them sharply felt, but especially Ñico López and Juan Manuel Márquez. Other combatants, who for their bravery and moral qualities had acquired great prestige among the troops, also lost their lives during this first year. Among them we can mention Nano and Julio Díaz—not brothers—both of whom died in the battle of El Uvero; Ciro Redondo, who died in the battle of Mar Verde; and Captain Soto, who died in the battle of San Lorenzo. In the cities, among the many martyrs of our struggle, we have to mention the greatest loss to the revolution up to that time: Frank País, who died in Santiago de Cuba.

To the list of military feats in the Sierra Maestra, must be added the work carried out by the *Llano* forces in the cities. In each of the nation's principal towns, groups were fighting against Batista's regime, but the two focal points of the struggle were Havana and Santiago.

Comprehensive communication between the *Llano* and the *Sierra* was always lacking, due to two fundamental factors: the geographical isolation of the Sierra Maestra, and all types of tactical and strategic differences between the two groups. This situation arose from differing social and political conceptions. The Sierra Maestra was isolated because of geographical conditions and because the army's cordon was sometimes extremely difficult to break through.

In this brief sketch of the country's struggle over the course of a year, we must mention the activities—generally fruitless and culminating in unfortunate results—of other groups of combatants.

On March 13, 1957, the Revolutionary Directorate attacked the presidential palace in an attempt to bring Batista to justice. A fine handful of fighters fell in that action, headed by the president of the Federation of University Students—a great combatant and a symbol of our youth, "Manzanita" Echeverría.

A few months later, in May, a landing was attempted. It had probably already been betrayed before setting out from Miami, since it was financed by the traitor Prío. It resulted in a massacre of almost all its participants. This was the *Corinthia* expedition, led by Calixto Sánchez, who was killed together with his compañeros, by Cowley, the assassin from northern Oriente, who was later brought to justice by members of our movement.

Combat groups were established in the Escambray, some of them led by the July 26 Movement and others by the Revolutionary Directorate. The latter groups were originally led by a member of the Revolutionary Directorate who later betrayed them and then the revolution itself—Gutíerrez Menoyo, today in exile. The combatants loyal to the Revolutionary Directorate formed a separate column that was later directed by Commander Chomón; those who remained set up the Second National Front of the Escambray.

Small cells were formed in the Cristal and Baracoa mountains, which at times were half guerrilla, half cattle-rustler; Raúl cleaned them out when he went there with Column 6. Another incident in the armed struggle of that period was the uprising at the Cienfuegos naval base on September 5, 1957, led by Lieutenant San Román, who was assassinated when the coup failed. The base was not supposed to rebel on its own, but this was not a spontaneous action. It was part of a large underground movement among the armed forces, led by a group of so-called pure military men (those untainted by the dictatorship's crimes), which—today it is obvious—was penetrated by Yankee imperialism. For some obscure motive, the uprising was postponed to a later date, but the Cienfuegos naval base did not receive the order in time. Unable to stop the uprising, they decided to go through with it. At first they gained control but they committed the tragic error of not marching for the Escambray mountains—only a few minutes away from Cienfuegos—at the moment when they controlled the entire city and had the means to form a solid front in the mountains.

National and local leaders of the July 26 Movement participated. So did the people; at least they shared in the enthusiasm that led to the revolt, and some of them took up arms. This may have created a moral obligation on the part of the uprising's leaders, tying them even closer to the conquered city; but the course of events developed as in every uprising of its type, which history has seen and will see again.

Obviously, the underestimation of the guerrilla struggle by academy-oriented military men played an important role, as did their lack of faith in the guerrilla movement as an expression of the people's struggle. The conspirators, probably assuming that without the aid of their comrades-in-arms they were lost, decided to fight to the death within the narrow boundaries of a city, their backs to the sea, until they were virtually annihilated by the superior forces of the enemy, which had easily mobilized its troops and converged on Cienfuegos. The July 26 Movement, participating as an unarmed ally, could not have changed the scenario, even if its leaders had seen the end result clearly, which they did not. The lesson for the future is that he who has the strength dictates the strategy.

The large-scale killing of civilians, repeated failures, murders committed by the dictatorship in different points of the struggle, indicate that guerrilla action on favorable terrain is the best expression of popular struggle against a despotic, still-strong government, that it is the least painful for the children of the people. After the guerrilla force was established, we could count our losses on our fingers—compañeros of outstanding courage and resolve in battle, to be sure. In the cities, however, not only the resolute died, but so did many among their followers who were not totally committed revolutionaries, or who were innocent of any involvement at all. They were more vulnerable in the face of repressive action.

By the end of this first year of struggle, a general uprising throughout the country was on the horizon. Acts of sabotage — ranging from the well planned and technically executed, to the trivial, hot-headed terrorist acts carried out on individual impulse — left a tragic toll of innocent deaths and sacrifices among the best combatants, without any real advantage to the people's cause.

We were consolidating our military situation and the territory we occupied was extensive. We were in a state of armed truce with Batista; his men did not go up into the Sierra Maestra and we hardly ever went down. They made their encirclement as effective as they could, but our troops still managed to evade them.

By the end of the year, in organizational terms, our guerrilla army had developed sufficiently to have an elementary infrastructure regarding provisions, certain minimal industrial services, hospitals, and communications services.

The problems of each guerrilla fighter were very simple. To subsist as an individual, they needed small amounts of food and certain indispensable items like clothes and medicine. To subsist as a guerrilla, that is, as part of an armed force in struggle, they needed arms and ammunition. For their political development, they needed information. To assure these minimal necessities is precisely why a communications and information apparatus was required.

In the beginning, the small guerrilla units, some 20 men, would eat a meager ration of Sierra Maestra vegetables, chicken soup in the case of a banquet, and sometimes the peasants provided a pig, for which they were paid religiously. As the guerrilla force grew and groups of new "pre-guerrillas" were trained, more provisions were needed. The Sierra Maestra peasants did not have cattle and theirs was generally a subsistence diet. They depended on the sale of their coffee to buy any processed items they needed, such as salt, which did not exist in the Sierra Maestra. As an initial measure, we arranged with certain peasants that they should plant specific crops — beans, corn, rice, etc. — which we guaranteed to purchase. At the same time, we agreed on terms with some merchants in nearby towns for the supply of foodstuffs and equipment. Mule teams were organized, belonging to the guerrilla forces.

As for medicines, we obtained them in the cities, not always in the quantity or quality we needed; but at least we were able to maintain some kind of functioning apparatus for their acquisition.

It was difficult to bring arms up from the *Llano*. To the natural difficulties of geographical isolation were added the requirements of the city forces themselves, and their reluctance to deliver arms to the guerrillas. Fidel was constantly involved in sharp discussions in an effort to secure the arrival of equipment. The only substantial shipment made to us during that first year of struggle, except for what the combatants brought with them, was what remained of the arms used in the attack on the presidential palace. These were transported with the cooperation of a big landowner and timber merchant of the zone, a man named Babún whom I have already mentioned.

Our ammunition was limited in quantity and lacking the necessary variety. It was impossible, however, for us to manufacture it ourselves or even to recharge cartridges in this first period, except for .38 bullets, which our gunsmith would recharge with a little gunpowder, and some of the .30-06 bullets to use in the single-shot rifles, since they caused the semiautomatics to jam and impeded their proper functioning.

Concerning the organization the life in the camps and communications, certain sanitary regulations were established, and in this period the first hospitals were organized. One was set up in the zone under my command, in an inaccessible place that offered relative security to the wounded, since it was invisible from the air. But it was in the heart of a dense woods, and dampness made it unhealthy for the wounded and sick. This hospital was organized by compañero Sergio del Valle. The doctors Martínez Páez, Vallejo, and Piti Fajardo organized similar hospitals in Fidel's column, but these were only improved during the second year of the struggle.

The troop's equipment needs, such as cartridge boxes, belts, backpacks, and shoes were covered by a small leather-goods workshop set up in our zone. I took the first army cap we turned out to Fidel, bursting with pride. Later, I became the butt of everyone's joke; they claimed it was the cap of a *guagüero* [bus driver], a word unknown to me until then. The only one who showed me any mercy was one of Batista's councillors from Manzanillo, who was visiting the camp to arrange to join our forces and who took it with him as a souvenir.

Our most important industrial installation was a forge and armory, where defective arms were repaired and bombs, mines, and the famous M-26s [small bombs] were made. At first, the mines were made of tin cans and we filled them with material from the unexploded bombs frequently dropped by enemy planes. These mines were very defective. Furthermore, their firing pins, for striking the detonator, frequently missed. Later, a compañero had the idea of using the whole bomb in major attacks, removing the detonator and replacing it with a loaded shotgun; we pulled the trigger from a distance using a cord, and it exploded. Afterward, we perfected the system, making special fuses of metal alloy and electric detonators. These gave better results. Although we began this development, Fidel gave it real impetus; later, in his new operations center, Raúl created stronger industries than those we had during the first year of the war.

To please the smokers among us, we set up a cigar factory; the cigars we made were terrible but, lacking better, they tasted glorious.

The butcher shop of our army was supplied with cattle confiscated from informers and big landowners. We shared equitably, one part for the peasant population and one part for our troop.

As for disseminating our ideas, first we started a small newspaper, *El Cubano Libre*, in memory of those heroes of the woods [the *Mambís*]. Three or four issues came out under our supervision; it was later edited by Luis Orlando Rodríguez, and subsequently Carlos Franqui gave it new impetus. We had a mimeograph machine brought up to us from the *Llano*, on which the paper was printed.

By the end of the first year and the beginning of the second, we had a small radio transmitter. The first regular broadcasts [of Radio Rebelde] were made in February 1958. Our only listeners were Palencho, a peasant who lived on the hill facing the station, and Fidel, who was visiting our camp in preparation for the attack on Pino del Agua. He listened to it on our own receiver. Little by little the technical quality of the broadcasts improved. Then it was taken over by Column 1 and by the end of the campaign, in December 1958, had become one of the highest "rating" Cuban stations.

All these small advances, including our equipment—such as a winch and some generators, laboriously carried up to the Sierra Maestra to have electric light—were due to our own connections. To confront our difficulties we had to begin creating our own network of communications and information. In this respect, Lidia Doce played an important part in my column, Clodomira [Acosta] in Fidel's.

Help came not only from people in neighboring villages; even the urban bourgeoisie contributed equipment to the guerrilla struggle. Our lines of communication reached as far as the towns of Contramaestre, Palma, Bueycito, Minas de Bueycito, Estrada Palma, Yara, Bayamo, Manzanillo, and Guisa; these places served as relay stations. Goods were then carried by mules along hidden trails in the Sierra Maestra up to our positions. At times, those among us who were in training but not yet armed, went down to the nearest towns, such as Yao or Minas, with some of our armed men, or they would go to well-stocked stores in the district. They carried supplies up to our refuge on their backs. The only item we never — or almost never — lacked in the Sierra Maestra was coffee. At times we lacked salt, one of the most important foods for survival, whose virtues we became aware of only when it was scarce.

When we began to broadcast from our own transmitter, the undeniable existence of our troops and their determination to fight became known throughout the republic. Our links began to become more extensive and complex, even reaching Havana and Camagüey to the west, where we had important supply centers, and Santiago in the east.

Our information service developed in such a way that peasants in the zone immediately notified us of the presence not only of the army, but of any stranger. We could easily detain such a person to investigate their activities. Many army agents and informers, infiltrating the zone to scrutinize our lives and actions, were eliminated in this way.

We began to establish a legal service, but as of then no Sierra Maestra law had been promulgated.

Such was our organizational situation at the beginning of the last year of the war.

As for the political struggle, it was very complicated and contradictory. Batista's dictatorship was supported by a congress elected through so many frauds that it could count on a comfortable majority to do its bidding.

Certain dissident opinions—when there was no censorship— were allowed expression, but officials and official spokespeople had powerful voices, and the networks transmitted their calls for national unity throughout the island. Otto Meruelo's hysterical voice alternated with the pompous buffooneries of Pardo Llada and Conte Agüero. The latter, repeating in writing what he had broadcast, called on "brother Fidel" to accept coexistence with Batista's regime.

Opposition groups were varied and diverse, although as a common denominator most had the wish to take power (read public funds) for themselves. This brought in its wake a sordid internal struggle to win that victory. Batista's agents infiltrated all the groups and, at key moments, denounced any significant activities to the government. Although gangsterism and opportunism characterized these groups, they also had their martyrs, some of national repute. In effect, Cuban society was in such total disarray that brave and honest people were sacrificing their lives to maintain the comfortable existence of such personages as Prío Socarrás.

The Revolutionary Directorate took the path of insurrectional struggle, but their movement was independent of ours and they had their own line. The Popular Socialist Party (PSP) joined us in certain concrete activities, but mutual distrust hampered joint action and, fundamentally, the workers party did not clearly understand the role of the guerrilla force, or Fidel's personal role in our revolutionary struggle.

During a friendly discussion, I once made an observation to a PSP leader, which he later repeated to others as an accurate characterization of that period, "You are capable of creating cadres who can endure the most terrible tortures in jail, without uttering a word, but you can't create cadres who can take out a machine gun nest." As I saw it from my guerrilla vantage point, this was the consequence of a strategic conception: a determination to struggle against imperialism and the abuses of the exploiting classes, together with an inability to envisage the possibility of taking power. Later, some of their people — of guerrilla spirit — were to join us, but by then the end of the armed struggle was near; its influence on them was slight.

Within our own movement there were two quite clearly defined tendencies, which we have already referred to as the *Sierra* and the *Llano*. Differences over strategic concepts separated us. The *Sierra* was already confident of being able to carry out the guerrilla struggle, to spread it to other places and, from the countryside, to encircle the cities held by the dictatorship, and by strangulation and attrition, destroy the entire apparatus of the regime.

The *Llano* took an ostensibly more revolutionary position, that of armed struggle in all towns, culminating in a general strike which would topple Batista and allow the prompt seizure of power.

This position was only apparently more revolutionary, because in that period the political development of the *Llano* compañeros was not complete and their conception of a general strike was too narrow. A general strike called the following year without warning, in secrecy, without prior political preparation or mass action, would lead to the defeat of April 9, [1958].

These two tendencies were represented in the national committee of the movement, which changed as the struggle developed. In the preparatory stage, until Fidel left for Mexico, the national committee consisted of Fidel, Raúl, Faustino Pérez, Pedro Miret, Ñico López, Armando Hart, Pepe Suárez, Pedro Aguilera, Luis Bonito, Jesús Montané, Melba Hernández, and Haydée Santamaría — if my information is correct and considering my personal participation at that time was very limited and documentation is scarce. Later, for reasons of incompatibility, Pepe Suárez, Pedro Aguilera, and Luis Bonito withdrew. While we were preparing for the struggle [in Mexico], the following people joined the committee: Mario Hidalgo, Aldo Santamaría, Carlos Franqui, Gustavo Arcos, and Frank País.

Of all the compañeros named, Fidel and Raúl alone went to the Sierra Maestra and remained there during the first year. Faustino Pérez, a *Granma* expeditionary, was put in charge of actions in the city. Pedro Miret was jailed a few hours before we were to leave Mexico. He remained there until the following year, when he arrived in Cuba with an arms shipment. Ñico López died only a few days after the landing. Armando Hart was jailed at the end of that year (or early the next). Jesús Montané was jailed after the landing, as was Mario Hidalgo. Melba Hernández and Haydée Santamaría worked in the cities. Aldo Santamaría and Carlos Franqui joined the struggle in the Sierra Maestra the following year. Gustavo Arcos remained in Mexico, in charge of political liaison and supplies. Frank País, assigned to head up actions in Santiago, was killed in July 1957.

Later, the following people joined the leadership body within the *Sierra*: Celia Sánchez, who stayed with us throughout 1958; Vilma Espín, who was working in Santiago and finished the war with Raúl Castro's column; Marcelo Fernández, coordinator of the movement, who replaced Faustino after the April 9 strike and stayed with us only a few weeks, since his work was in the towns; René Ramos Latour, assigned to organizing the *Llano* militia, came up to the Sierra Maestra after the April 9 failure and during the second year of the struggle died heroically as a commander; David Salvador, in charge of the labor movement, on which he left the imprint of his opportunist and divisive actions—he was later to betray the revolution and is now in prison. Some of the *Sierra* combatants, such as [Juan] Almeida, were to join the national leadership some time later.

As can be seen, during this stage the *Llano* compañeros constituted the majority. Their political backgrounds, which had not really been influenced by the revolutionary process, led them to favor a certain type of "civil" action, and to a kind of resistance to the caudillo they saw in Fidel and to the "militarist" faction represented by us in the Sierra Maestra. The differences were already apparent, but they were not yet strong enough to provoke the turbulent discussions that characterized the second year of the war.

It is important to point out that those fighting the dictatorship in the *Sierra* and the *Llano* were able to maintain opinions on tactics that were at times diametrically opposed, without this leading to abandoning the insurrectional struggle. Their revolutionary spirit continued to deepen until the moment when — victory in hand, followed by our first experiences in the struggle against imperialism — they all came together [as the Integrated Revolutionary Organizations in 1961] in a strong, party-like organization, led indisputably by Fidel. This group then joined with the Revolutionary Directorate and the Popular Socialist Party to form the United Party of the Socialist Revolution (PURS) [in 1963]. In the face of external pressure from outside our movement and attempts to divide or infiltrate it, we always presented a common front. Even those compañeros who in the period we are describing viewed the picture of the Cuban revolution with imperfect perspective were wary of opportunists.

When Felipe Pazos, invoking the name of the July 26 Movement, sought to appropriate for himself, and for the most corrupt oligarchic interests of Cuba, the positions offered by the Miami Pact, including the position of provisional president, the entire movement united solidly against this stand, and supported the letter Fidel Castro sent to the organizations involved in the struggle against Batista. We reproduce this historic document here in its entirety. It is dated December 14, 1957, and was copied out by Celia Sánchez, since conditions of that period made it impossible to print....

From: *Reminiscences of the Cuban Revolutionary War* by Ernesto Che Guevara

THE FINAL OFFENSIVE AND THE BATTLE OF SANTA CLARA
MAY–DECEMBER 1958

[The general strike of] April 9 [1958] was a resounding defeat that never endangered the regime's stability. Furthermore, after that tragic date, the government was able to transfer troops and gradually place them in Oriente province, spreading its destruction to the Sierra Maestra. More and more our defense had to be from within the Sierra Maestra, and the government kept increasing the number of regiments it placed in front of our positions, until there were 10,000 men. With these forces it began the May 25 offensive in the town of Las Mercedes, which was our forward position.

There, Batista's army gave proof of its ineffectiveness in combat, and we showed our lack of resources: 200 working rifles to fight against 10,000 weapons of all sorts — an enormous disadvantage. Our troops fought bravely for two days, with odds of one against 10 or 15, moreover fighting against mortars, tanks, and the air force, until the small group was forced to abandon the town. It was commanded by Captain Ángel Verdecia, who one month later would die in battle courageously.

By that time, Fidel Castro had received a letter from the traitor Eulogio Cantillo, who, true to his charlatan's politicking nature, wrote as the enemy's chief of operations to the rebel leader, saying that the offensive would be launched in any case, but that "The Man" (Fidel) should take care to await the final result. The offensive, in fact, ran its course, and in two and a half months of hard fighting, the enemy lost over 1,000 men, counting dead, wounded, prisoners, and deserters. They also left 600 weapons in our hands, including a tank, 12 mortars, 12 tripod machine guns, over 200 submachine guns, and countless automatic weapons; also, an enormous amount of ammunition and equipment of all sorts, and 450 prisoners, who were handed over to the Red Cross when the campaign ended.

Batista's army came out of that last offensive in the Sierra Maestra with its spine broken, but it had not yet been defeated. The struggle continued. It was then that the final strategy was established, attacking at three points: Santiago de Cuba, which had been under a flexible siege; Las Villas, where I was to go; and Pinar del Río, at the other end of the island, where Camilo Cienfuegos was to march as commander of Column 2, named "Antonio Maceo" in memory of the historic invasion by the great leader of 1895, who crossed the length of Cuban territory with epic actions, culminating at Mantua. Camilo Cienfuegos was not able to fulfill the second part of his program, as the exigencies of the war forced him to remain in Las Villas.

Once the regiments assaulting the Sierra Maestra had been wiped out, the front had returned to its normal intensity, and our troops had increased their strength and morale, it was decided to begin marching on the central province of Las Villas. My orders specified our main strategic task: to systematically cut off communications between both extremes of the island. I was also ordered to establish relations with all political groups that might be operating in the mountains of the region, and I was given broad powers to govern my assigned area militarily.

We were to set off by truck on August 30, 1958, with these

instructions and believing the trip would take four days. Then an unexpected accident disrupted our plans. A pickup truck was arriving that night, carrying uniforms and gasoline for the otherwise prepared vehicles. A cargo of arms also arrived, by air, at an airstrip close to the road. But the plane was sighted just as it landed, even though it was dark, and the airstrip was bombed systematically from 8 p.m. until 5 a.m. At that point, we ourselves burned the plane to prevent it falling into enemy hands or having the bombardment continue by day, with even worse results. Enemy troops advanced on the airstrip, intercepting the pickup truck carrying the gasoline and leaving us on foot.

So it was that we began the march on August 31, without trucks or horses, hoping to find them after crossing the highway from Manzanillo to Bayamo. In fact, having crossed it we found the trucks, but also—on the first day of September—we encountered a fierce hurricane that made all roads impassable except for the central highway, the only paved road in this region of Cuba, forcing us to give up on vehicle transport. From that moment on we had to use horses, or walk. We were loaded down with a lot of ammunition, a bazooka with 40 shells, and everything necessary for a long march and for rapidly setting up camp.

Days passed, and it was already becoming difficult, even though we were in the friendly territory of Oriente: crossing over-flowing rivers and streams that had become rivers, struggling with difficulty to prevent our ammunition, arms, and shells from getting wet; looking for horses and leaving tired horses behind; avoiding inhabited zones as we moved away from the eastern province.

We walked through difficult, flooded terrain, suffering the attacks of mosquito swarms that made periods of rest unbearable, eating little and poorly, drinking water from swampy rivers or simply from swamps. Each day of travel became longer and truly horrible. A week after leaving camp, by the time we crossed the Jobabo River, which marks the border between Oriente and Camagüey provinces, our forces were greatly weakened. This river, like all the previous ones and those we would cross later, was flooded. We were also feeling the effects of the lack of footwear among our troops, many of whom were walking barefoot through the mud of southern Camagüey.

On the night of September 9, as we were approaching a place known as La Federal, our forward guard fell into an enemy ambush, and two valuable compañeros were killed. But the most lamentable consequence was being noticed by the enemy forces, who from then on gave us no respite. After a brief clash, the small garrison there surrendered and we took four prisoners. Now we had to march very carefully, since the air force knew our approximate course. One or two days later, we reached a place known as Laguna Grande, together with Camilo's force—much better equipped than ours. The area stands out for its extraordinary number of mosquitoes, which made it absolutely impossible for us to rest without a mosquito net, and not all of us had one.

These were days of tiring marches through desolate expanses of only water and mud. We were hungry, thirsty, and could hardly advance because our legs felt like lead and the weapons were tremendously heavy. We continued advancing with the better horses Camilo had left us when his column took their trucks, but we had to give them up near the Macareño sugar mill. The guides they were supposed to send us did not arrive and we set off on the adventure as we were.

Our forward guard clashed with an enemy outpost in a place called Cuatro Compañeros and the exhausting battle began. It was daybreak, and with great effort we managed to gather a large part of our troop in the biggest woods in the area. But the army was advancing along its edges and we had to fight hard to make it possible for some of our men, who had fallen behind, to cross some railroad tracks into the woods. The air force then sighted us and the B-26s, the C-47s, the big C-3 reconnaissance planes, and the light planes began bombing an area no more than 200 meters wide. Finally, we withdrew, leaving one man killed by a bomb and carrying several wounded, including Captain Silva, who went through the rest of the invasion with a broken shoulder.

The picture the following day was less desolate, since many of those who had fallen behind showed up, and we managed to gather the whole troop, minus the 10 men who were to join Camilo's column and with him get to the northern front of Las Villas province, in Yaguajay.

Despite the difficulties, we were never without the encouragement of the peasants. We always found someone who would serve as a guide, or who would give us the food without which we could not go on. Naturally, it was not the unanimous support of the whole people we had enjoyed in Oriente, but there was always someone who helped us. At times we were reported to the enemy as soon as we crossed a farm, but that was not because peasants were acting directly against us. Rather, their living conditions made these people slaves of the landowners and, fearful of losing their daily subsistence, they would report to their master that we had passed through the region. The latter would take charge of graciously informing the military authorities.

One afternoon we were listening on our field radio to a report by General Francisco Tabernilla Dolz, who with the typical arrogance of a thug was announcing that Che Guevara's hordes had been destroyed. He was giving extensive details about the dead, the wounded, names, and all sorts of things — based on items taken from our backpacks after that disastrous encounter with the enemy a few days earlier. All this was mixed with false information cooked up by the army's high command. News of our passing produced great merriment among our troop, but pessimism was getting hold of them little by little. Hunger and thirst, exhaustion, feeling impotent against the enemy forces closing in on us, and more than anything, the terrible foot disease the peasants call *mazamorra*—which turned each step our soldiers took into an intolerable torment—had made us an army of shadows. It was difficult, very difficult, to advance. Our troop's physical condition worsened day by day, and the meals—today yes, tomorrow no, the next day maybe—in no way helped alleviate the misery we were suffering.

We spent the hardest days besieged in the vicinity of the Baraguá sugar mill in pestilent swamps, without a drop of drinking water; attacked constantly by the air force; not a single horse to carry the weakest across barren marshes; our shoes totally destroyed by the muddy seawater; and plants injuring our bare feet. Our situation was really disastrous when, with difficulty, we broke out of the encirclement at Baraguá and reached the famous Júcaro–Morón trail, an historically evocative place, the scene of bloody fighting between patriots and Spaniards during the war of independence.

We had no time to recover even a little when a new downpour, bad weather, enemy attacks, or reports of their presence forced us to march on. The troop was increasingly tired and disheartened. When the situation was most tense, however, when insults, pleas, and sharp remarks were the only way to get the weary men to advance, a sight far away in the distance lit up their faces and instilled a new spirit in the guerrillas. That sight was a blue streak to the west, the blue streak of Las Villas mountain range, seen for the first time by our men. From that moment on, the same or similar hardships became more bearable and everything seemed easier. We slipped through the last encirclement by swimming across the Júcaro River, which divides the provinces of Camagüey and Las Villas, and it already seemed that a new light was illuminating us.

Two days later we were in the heart of the Trinidad–Sancti Spíritus mountain range, safe, ready to begin the next stage of the war. We rested for another two days; we had to be on our way immediately and prepare ourselves to prevent the elections scheduled for November 3. We had reached the mountains of Las Villas on October 16. Time was short and the task was enormous. Camilo was doing his part in the north, sowing fear among the dictatorship's men.

Our task, upon arriving for the first time in the Escambray mountains, was clearly defined: we had to harass the dictatorship's military apparatus, above all its communications; and, as an immediate goal, we had to prevent the elections from taking place. But this work was made difficult because time was scarce, and because of the disunity among the revolutionary forces, which translated into internal quarrels that cost us dearly, including human lives.

We were supposed to attack the neighboring towns to prevent the elections, and plans were elaborated to do this simultaneously in the cities of Cabaiguán, Fomento, and Sancti Spíritus, in the rich plains of the center of the island. Meanwhile, the small garrison at Güinía de Miranda — in the mountains — surrendered; later the Banao garrison was attacked, with few results. The days prior to November 3, the date of the elections, were extraordinarily busy. Our columns were mobilized everywhere, almost totally preventing voters in those areas from going to the polls. Camilo Cienfuegos's troops in the northern part of the province paralyzed the electoral farce. Basically, from the transport of Batista's soldiers to commercial traffic, everything stood still.

There was practically no voting in Oriente; the percentage was a little higher in Camagüey; and in the western region, in spite of everything, mass abstention was evident. This abstention was achieved spontaneously in Las Villas, as there had not been time to synchronize the passive resistance of the masses with the activity of the guerrillas.

In Oriente, successive battles were taking place on the first and second fronts, as well as on the third, with the "Antonio Guiteras" Column 9 relentlessly exerting pressure on Santiago de Cuba, the provincial capital. Except for municipal seats, the government had nothing left in Oriente.

The situation was also becoming very serious in Las Villas, with intensified attacks on communications. On arrival, we completely changed the system of struggle in the cities; we rapidly sent the best militia members from the cities to the training camp to receive instruction in sabotage, which proved effective in urban areas.

During the months of November and December 1958, we gradually closed the highways. Captain Silva totally blocked the highway from Trinidad to Sancti Spíritus, and the island's central highway was seriously damaged when the bridge across the Tuinicú River was dynamited, although it did not collapse completely. The central railroad was blocked at several points; moreover, the southern route had been cut by the second front and the northern route had been closed by Camilo Cienfuegos's troops. The island was divided into two parts. The region most in upheaval, Oriente, received aid from the government only by air and sea, and this became increasingly insecure. The symptoms of the enemy's disintegration were increasing.

An extremely intense campaign for revolutionary unity had to be carried out in the Escambray mountains, because already operating there was a group led by Commander [Eloy] Gutiérrez Menoyo (Second National Front of the Escambray), another of the Revolutionary Directorate (led by commanders Faure Chomón and Rolando Cubela), another smaller one of the Authentic Organization, another of the Popular Socialist Party (commanded by [Félix] Torres), and us. In other words, there were five different organizations operating under different commands and in the same province. After laborious talks I had to have with their respective leaders, we reached a series of agreements and it was possible to go on to form a more or less common front.

From December 16 onward, the systematic cutting off of bridges and all kinds of communications had made it very difficult for the dictatorship to defend its forward positions and even those on the central highway. Early that day, the bridge across the Falcón River, on the central highway, was destroyed, and communications between Havana and the cities to the east of Santa Clara, the capital of Las Villas province, were virtually cut off. Also, a number of towns — the southernmost being Fomento — were besieged and attacked by our forces. The commander of the city defended his position more or less effectively for several days. Despite the air force's punishment of our Rebel Army, the dictatorship's demoralized troops would not advance overland to support their comrades. Realizing that all resistance was useless, they surrendered, and more than 100 rifles joined the forces of freedom.

Without giving the enemy any respite, we decided to paralyze the central highway immediately, and on December 21 we simultaneously attacked Cabaiguán and Guayos, both on the central highway. The latter surrendered in a few hours, and during the following days, so did Cabaiguán with its 90 soldiers. (The surrender of the garrisons was negotiated on the political basis of letting the soldiers go free, on the condition that they leave the liberated territory. In this manner, they were given the opportunity to surrender their weapons and save themselves.) Cabaiguán once again proved the dictatorship's ineffectiveness, as it never sent infantry units to reinforce those under siege.

In the northern region of Las Villas, Camilo Cienfuegos was attacking several towns, which he was subduing at the same time as he was laying siege to Yaguajay, the last bastion of the dictatorship's troops. Yaguajay was under the command of a captain of Chinese ancestry who resisted for 11 days, immobilizing the revolutionary troops in the region. At the same time our troops were already advancing along the central highway toward Santa Clara, the provincial capital.

After Cabaiguán had fallen, we set out—in active collaboration with the forces of the Revolutionary Directorate—to attack Placetas, which surrendered after only one day of struggle. After taking Placetas, we liberated in rapid succession Remedios and Caibarién on the northern coast, the latter an important port. The picture was becoming gloomy for the dictatorship because, in addition to continuous victories scored in Oriente, the Second National Front of the Escambray was defeating small garrisons, and Camilo Cienfuegos controlled the north.

When the enemy withdrew from Camajuaní without offering resistance, we were ready to launch the definitive attack on the capital of Las Villas province. (Santa Clara is the hub of the island's central plain, with 150,000 inhabitants, it is the center of the railroad system and all communications in the country.) It is surrounded by small, bare hills, which were previously occupied by the troops of the dictatorship.

At the time of the attack, our forces had considerably increased our weaponry, as we had taken several positions and some heavy weapons, which were lacking ammunition. We had a bazooka without shells, and we had to fight against some 10 tanks. We also knew that for us to fight most effectively, we had to reach the city's populous neighborhoods, where a tank is much less effective.

While the troops of the Revolutionary Directorate were taking the Rural Guard's garrison No. 31, we set about besieging almost all of Santa Clara's fortified positions. Fundamentally, however, our fight was focused against the guards of the armored train stationed at the start of the Camajuaní road. The army, which was well equipped, tenaciously defended these positions.

On December 29, we began the struggle. The university served as our operations base at first. Later, we established our headquarters closer to the city's downtown area. Our men were fighting against troops supported by armored units and were forcing them to flee, although many paid for their boldness with their lives. The dead and wounded began to fill the improvised cemeteries and hospitals.

I remember an episode that highlights the spirit of our forces in those final days. I had admonished a compañero because he was sleeping in the midst of battle, and he replied that he had been disarmed for accidentally firing his weapon. I responded with habitual dryness, "Get yourself another rifle by going disarmed to the front line… if you're up to it." In Santa Clara, while speaking to the wounded in the Sangre Hospital, a dying man touched my hand and said, "Remember, commander? In Remedios you sent me to find a weapon… and I earned it here." He was the combatant who had accidentally fired his weapon. He died a few minutes later, I think content for having proven his courage. Such was our Rebel Army.

The hills of Cápiro continued to resist, and we continued fighting there the whole day of December 30, at the same time gradually taking different points in the city. By then, communications between the center of Santa Clara and the armored train had been cut off. Those in the train, seeing they were surrounded on the hills of Cápiro, tried to escape by rail with all their magnificent cargo. Arriving at the spur we had already destroyed, the locomotive and some carriages were derailed. A very interesting battle began, in which our Molotov cocktails forced the men out of the armored train. They were very well protected but only willing to fight at a distance, from comfortable positions, against a virtually unarmed enemy, in the style of the colonizers against the Indians of the North American west. Assaulted by men who from nearby positions and adjoining carriages threw bottles of burning gasoline, the train became a veritable oven for the soldiers, thanks to its armored plating. In a few hours, the whole lot surrendered with their 22 carriages, their antiaircraft guns, their machine guns of the same type, and their fabulous quantity of ammunition (fabulous, of course, compared with our meager supply).

We had been able to take the power station and the city's whole northwest side. We went on the air to announce that Santa Clara was almost in the hands of the revolution. In the announcement, which I made as commander-in-chief of the armed forces in Las Villas, I remember I had the sorrow of informing the Cuban people of the death of Captain Roberto Rodríguez, "Vaquerito," small in stature and years and leader of the "suicide squad," who had played with death a thousand and one times fighting for freedom. The "suicide squad" was an example of revolutionary morale, and only selected volunteers joined it. But whenever a man died—and that happened in every battle—and when the new aspirant was named, those not chosen would be grief-stricken and even cry. Strange to see those seasoned, noble figures showing their youth in their tears of despair, because they did not have the honor of being in the front line of combat and death.

The police station fell next, surrendering the tanks that defended it. And in rapid succession No. 31 garrison surrendered to Commander Cubela, while the jail, the courthouse, the provincial government palace, and the Grand Hotel—where snipers on the 10th floor had kept up fire almost until the end of combat—surrendered to our forces.

At that moment, only the Leoncio Vidal garrison, the largest fortress in central Cuba, had not surrendered. But by January 1, 1959, there were already growing signs of weakness among the forces defending it. That morning, we sent captains [Antonio] Núñez Jiménez and [Alfonso] Rodríguez de la Vega to negotiate the surrender of the garrison.

Reports were contradictory and extraordinary: Batista had fled that day, leaving the high command of the armed forces in complete disarray. Our two delegates established radio contact with

[General Eulogio] Cantillo, telling him of the offer of surrender. But he indicated he could not accept because it constituted an ultimatum, and because he had taken over command of the army in accordance with precise instructions from the leader Fidel Castro. We contacted Fidel immediately, telling him the news, but giving our opinion of Cantillo's treacherous attitude — an opinion with which he absolutely agreed. (In those decisive hours, Cantillo let all the main figures in Batista's government escape. His attitude was even worse considering he was an officer who had contacted us; we had trusted him as a military man of honor.)

The results that followed are known to everyone: Castro's refusal to recognize Cantillo's authority; Fidel's order to march on the city of Havana; Colonel Barquín seizing command of the army after leaving the Isle of Pines prison; the seizure of Camp Columbia by Camilo Cienfuegos and of La Cabaña fortress by our Column 8; and the final installation, within a few days, of Fidel Castro as prime minister of the provisional government. All this belongs to the country's present political history.

We are now in a position in which we are much more than the simple instruments of one nation. We are now the hope of the unredeemed Americas. All eyes — those of the great oppressors and those of the hopeful — are firmly on us. In great measure, the development of the popular movements in Latin America depends on the future stance that we take, on our capacity to resolve so many problems. And every step we take is being observed by the ever-watchful eyes of the big creditor and by the optimistic eyes of our brothers and sisters in Latin America.

With our feet planted firmly on the ground, we are beginning to labor and produce our first revolutionary works; we confront the first difficulties. But what is Cuba's main problem if not the same as all of Latin America, the same even as enormous Brazil with its millions of square kilometers and with its land of marvels that is a whole continent? The one-crop economy. In Cuba, we are slaves to sugarcane—the umbilical cord that binds us to the large northern market. We must diversify our agricultural production, stimulate industry, and ensure that our minerals and agricultural products, and—in the near future—our industrial production, go to the markets that are best suited for us and by our own methods of transportation.

The government's first big battle will be the agrarian reform, which will be audacious, thorough, but flexible. It will destroy the large estates in Cuba, although not Cuba's means of production. It will be a battle that will absorb a great part of the strength of the people and the government during the coming years. The land will be given free to the peasant. Landowners who prove that they came by their holdings honestly will be compensated with long-term bonds. But the peasantry will also be given technical assistance; there will be guaranteed markets for the products of the soil. And production will be channeled with a broad national sense of development in conjunction with the great battle for agrarian reform, so that within a short time the infant Cuban industries can compete with the monstrous ones of the countries where capitalism has reached its highest level of development. Simultaneously with the creation of the new domestic market that the agrarian reform will bring about, and the distribution of new products to satisfy a growing market, there will arise the need to export some products and to have the adequate instrument to take them to this or that part of the world. That instrument will be a merchant fleet, which the already approved Maritime Development Law envisages.

With these elementary weapons, we Cubans will begin the struggle for our territory's total freedom. We all know it will not be easy, but we are all aware of the enormous historic responsibility of the July 26 Movement, of the Cuban revolution, of the nation in general, to be an example for all the peoples of Latin America, whom we must not disappoint.

Our friends of the indomitable continent can be sure that, if need be, we will struggle no matter what the economic consequence of our actions may be. And if the fight is taken further still, we shall struggle to the last drop of our rebel blood to make this land a sovereign republic, with the true attributes of a nation that is happy, democratic, and fraternal with its brothers and sisters of Latin America.

From: *Reminiscences of the Cuban Revolutionary War* by Ernesto Che Guevara

WHAT A GUERRILLA FIGHTER SHOULD BE

The following is an extract from *Guerrilla Warfare* by Ernesto Che Guevara.

THE GUERRILLA FIGHTER AS SOCIAL REFORMER

We have already identified the guerrilla fighter as one who shares the longing of the people for liberation and who, after peaceful means are exhausted, initiates the struggle and converts himself into an armed vanguard of the fighting people. From the commencement of the struggle the guerrilla is committed to destroying an unjust order and has the intention, more or less hidden, to replace the old with something new.

We have also said that in the current conditions, at least in America and in almost all countries with little economic development, the countryside offers ideal conditions for the struggle, thus the basic social claims that the guerrilla fighter will raise begin with changes in the structure of agrarian property.

In this period the banner of the struggle will be agrarian reform. At first this goal may or may not be completely defined in its extent and limits; it may simply refer to the age-old hunger of the peasant for the land he or she works or wishes to work.

The conditions in which the agrarian reform will be realized depend on the conditions that existed before the struggle began, and on the social depth of the struggle. But the guerrilla fighter, as the conscious element of the vanguard of the people, must display the moral conduct of a true priest of the desired reform. To the stoicism forced by the difficult conditions of warfare should be added an austerity born of rigid self-control that prevents a single excess, a single slip, whatever the circumstances. The guerrilla soldier should be an ascetic.[1]

Social relations will vary according to the development of the war. At the beginning it will not be possible to attempt any changes in the social order of the area.

Goods that cannot be paid for in cash will be paid for with bonds; and these should be redeemed at the first opportunity.

The peasant must always be given technical, economic, moral, and cultural assistance. The guerrilla fighter will be a kind of guardian angel who has dropped into the zone, always helping the poor and harassing the rich as little as possible in the first phases of the war. But as the war develops, contradictions will become sharper; the time will arrive when many of those who regarded the revolution sympathetically at the start will place themselves in a position diametrically opposed to it; and they will make the first move into battle against the popular forces. At that moment the guerrilla fighter should act to become the standard-bearer of the people's cause, punishing every betrayal with justice. Private property should acquire a social function in the war zones. In other words, excess land and livestock not essential for the maintenance of a wealthy family should pass into the hands of the people and be distributed equitably and fairly.

The right of the owners to receive payment for possessions used for the social good should always be respected; but this payment will be made in bonds ("bonds of hope," as they were called by our teacher, General Bayo, referring to the common interest that is thus established between debtor and creditor).

The land and property of notorious and active enemies of the revolution should pass immediately into the hands of the revolutionary forces. Furthermore, taking advantage of the heat of the war—those moments in which human fraternity reaches its greatest intensity—all kinds of cooperative work should be stimulated, as far as the mentality of the local people will allow.

As social reformers, guerrilla fighters should not only provide an example in their own lives, but should also constantly give an orientation on ideological issues, explaining what they know and what they wish to do at the right time. They should also make use of what they learn as the months or years of the war strengthen their revolutionary convictions, making them more radical as the potency of arms is demonstrated, as the outlook of the local people becomes a part of their spirit and of their own life, and as they understand the justice and the vital necessity of many changes, the theoretical importance of which they understood before, but perhaps not the practical urgency.

Very often this occurs because the initiators of a guerrilla war, or rather the directors of guerrilla warfare, are not those who have bent their backs day after day over the furrow. They understand the necessity for change in the social treatment of the peasants, but have never suffered this bitter treatment personally. What happens then (here, I am drawing on the Cuban experience and expanding on it) is a genuine interaction between those leaders, who by their actions teach the people the fundamental importance of the armed struggle, and the people themselves, who rise in rebellion and teach the leaders these practical necessities we are discussing. In this way, as a product of the interaction between the guerrilla fighters and their people, a progressive radicalization appears, further accentuating the revolutionary nature of the movement and giving it a national scope.

From: *Guerrilla Warfare* by Ernesto Che Guevara

"THE FINAL HOUR OF COLONIALISM HAS STRUCK."

★

ERNESTO CHE GUEVARA

NEW YORK

AT THE UNITED NATIONS
DECEMBER 11, 1964

Mr. President;
Distinguished delegates:

The delegation of Cuba to this Assembly, first of all, is pleased to fulfill the agreeable duty of welcoming the addition of three new nations to the important number of those that discuss the problems of the world here. We therefore greet, in the persons of their presidents and prime ministers, the peoples of Zambia, Malawi and Malta, and express the hope that from the outset these countries will be added to the group of Nonaligned countries that struggle against imperialism, colonialism and neocolonialism.

We also wish to convey our congratulations to the president of this Assembly [Alex Quaison-Sackey of Ghana], whose elevation to so high a post is of special significance since it reflects this new historic stage of resounding triumphs for the peoples of Africa, who up until recently were subject to the colonial system of imperialism. Today, in their immense majority these peoples have become sovereign states through the legitimate exercise of their self-determination. The final hour of colonialism has struck, and millions of inhabitants of Africa, Asia and Latin America rise to meet a new life and demand their unrestricted right to self-determination and to the independent development of their nations.

We wish you, Mr. President, the greatest success in the tasks entrusted to you by the member states.

Cuba comes here to state its position on the most important points of controversy and will do so with the full sense of responsibility that the use of this rostrum implies, while at the same time fulfilling the unavoidable duty of speaking clearly and frankly.

We would like to see this Assembly shake itself out of complacency and move forward. We would like to see the committees begin their work and not stop at the first confrontation. Imperialism wants to turn this meeting into a pointless oratorical tournament, instead of solving the serious problems of the world. We must prevent it from doing so. This session of the Assembly should not be remembered in the future solely by the number 19 that identifies it. Our efforts are directed to that end.

We feel that we have the right and the obligation to do so, because our country is one of the most constant points of friction. It is one of the places where the principles upholding the right of small countries to sovereignty are put to the test day by day, minute by minute. At the same time our country is one of the trenches of freedom in the world, situated a few steps away from US imperialism, showing by its actions, its daily example, that in the present conditions of humanity the peoples can liberate themselves and can keep themselves free.

Of course, there now exists a socialist camp that becomes stronger day by day and has more powerful weapons of struggle. But additional conditions are required for survival: the maintenance of internal unity, faith in one's own destiny, and the irrevocable decision to fight to the death for the defense of one's country and revolution. These conditions, distinguished delegates, exist in Cuba.

Of all the burning problems to be dealt with by this Assembly, one of special significance for us, and one whose solution we feel must be found first—so as to leave no doubt in the minds of anyone—is that of peaceful coexistence among states with different economic and social systems. Much progress has been made in the world in this field. But imperialism, particularly US imperialism, has attempted to make the world believe that peaceful coexistence is the exclusive right of the earth's great powers. We say here what our president said in Cairo, and what later was expressed in the declaration of the second conference of Heads of State or Government of nonaligned countries: that peaceful coexistence cannot be limited to the powerful countries if we want to ensure world peace. Peaceful coexistence must be exercised among all states, regardless of size, regardless of the previous historical relations that linked them, and regardless of the problems that may arise among some of them at a given moment.

At present, the type of peaceful coexistence to which we aspire is often violated. Merely because the Kingdom of Cambodia maintained a neutral attitude and did not bow to the machinations of US imperialism, it has been subjected to all kinds of treacherous and brutal attacks from the Yankee bases in South Vietnam.

Laos, a divided country, has also been the object of imperialist aggression of every kind. Its people have been massacred from the air. The conventions concluded at Geneva have been violated, and part of its territory is in constant danger of cowardly attacks by imperialist forces.

The Democratic Republic of Vietnam knows all this history of aggression as do few nations on earth. It has once again seen its frontier violated, has seen enemy bombers and fighter planes attack its installations and US warships, violating territorial waters, attack its naval posts. At this time, the threat hangs over the Democratic Republic of Vietnam that the US war makers may openly extend into its territory the war that for many years they have been waging against the people of South Vietnam. The Soviet Union and the People's Republic of China have given serious warnings to the United States. We are faced with a case in which world peace is in danger and, moreover, the lives of millions of human beings in this part of Asia are constantly threatened and subjected to the whim of the US invader.

Peaceful coexistence has also been brutally put to the test in Cyprus, due to pressures from the Turkish government and NATO, compelling the people and the government of Cyprus to make a heroic and firm stand in defense of their sovereignty.

In all these parts of the world, imperialism attempts to impose its version of what coexistence should be. It is the oppressed peoples in alliance with the socialist camp that must show them what true coexistence is, and it is the obligation of the United Nations to support them.

We must also state that it is not only in relations among sovereign states that the concept of peaceful coexistence needs to be precisely defined. As Marxists we have maintained that peaceful coexistence among nations does not encompass coexistence between the exploiters and the exploited, between the oppressors and the oppressed. Furthermore, the right to full independence from all forms of colonial oppression is a fundamental principle of this organization. That is why we express our solidarity with the colonial peoples of so-called Portuguese Guinea, Angola and Mozambique, who have been massacred for the crime of demanding their freedom. And we are prepared to help them to the extent of our ability in accordance with the Cairo declaration.

We express our solidarity with the people of Puerto Rico and their great leader, Pedro Albizu Campos, who, in another act of hypocrisy, has been set free at the age of 72, almost unable to speak, paralyzed, after spending a lifetime in jail. Albizu Campos is a symbol of the as yet unfree but indomitable Latin America. Years and years of prison, almost unbearable pressures in jail, mental torture, solitude, total isolation from his people and his family, the insolence of the conqueror and its lackeys in the land of his birth—nothing broke his will. The delegation of Cuba, on behalf of its people, pays a tribute of admiration and gratitude to a patriot who confers honor upon our America.

The United States for many years has tried to convert Puerto Rico into a model of hybrid culture: the Spanish language with English inflections, the Spanish language with hinges on its backbone—the better to bow down before the Yankee soldier. Puerto Rican soldiers have been used as cannon fodder in imperialist wars, as in Korea, and have even been made to fire at their own brothers, as in the massacre perpetrated by the US Army a few months ago against the unarmed people of Panama—one of the most recent crimes carried out by Yankee imperialism.* And yet, despite this assault on their will and their historical destiny, the people of Puerto Rico have preserved their culture, their Latin character, their national feelings, which in themselves give proof of the implacable desire for independence lying within the masses on that Latin American island.

We must also warn that the principle of peaceful coexistence does not encompass the right to mock the will of the peoples, as is happening in the case of so-called British Guiana. There the government of Prime Minister Cheddi Jagan has been the victim of every kind of pressure and maneuver, and independence has been delayed to gain time to find ways to flout the people's will and guarantee the docility of a new government, placed in power by covert means, in order to grant a castrated freedom to this country of the Americas. Whatever roads Guiana may be compelled to

---

* In January 1964 US forces opened fire on Panamanian students demonstrating in the US-occupied Canal Zone, sparking several days of street fighting. More than 20 Panamanians were killed and 300 were wounded.

follow to obtain independence, the moral and militant support of Cuba goes to its people.*

Furthermore, we must point out that the islands of Guadaloupe and Martinique have been fighting for a long time for self-government without obtaining it. This state of affairs must not continue.

Once again we speak out to put the world on guard against what is happening in South Africa. The brutal policy of apartheid is applied before the eyes of the nations of the world. The peoples of Africa are compelled to endure the fact that on the African continent the superiority of one race over another remains official policy, and that in the name of this racial superiority murder is committed with impunity. Can the United Nations do nothing to stop this?

I would like to refer specifically to the painful case of the Congo, unique in the history of the modern world, which shows how, with absolute impunity, with the most insolent cynicism, the rights of peoples can be flouted. The direct reason for all this is the enormous wealth of the Congo, which the imperialist countries want to keep under their control. In the speech he made during his first visit to the United Nations, compañero Fidel Castro observed that the whole problem of coexistence among peoples boils down to the wrongful appropriation of other peoples' wealth. He made the following statement: "End the philosophy of plunder and the philosophy of war will be ended as well."

But the philosophy of plunder has not only not ended, it is stronger than ever. And that is why those who used the name of the United Nations to commit the murder of Lumumba are

---

* Cheddi Jagan had become prime minister of British Guiana after the People's Progressive Party won the 1953 elections; shortly thereafter Britain suspended the constitution. Jagan was reelected in 1957 and 1961. In 1964 he was defeated in an election by Forbes Burnham. In 1966 Guiana won its independence.

today, in the name of the defense of the white race, murdering thousands of Congolese. How can we forget the betrayal of the hope that Patrice Lumumba placed in the United Nations? How can we forget the machinations and maneuvers that followed in the wake of the occupation of that country by UN troops, under whose auspices the assassins of this great African patriot acted with impunity? How can we forget, distinguished delegates, that the one who flouted the authority of the UN in the Congo — and not exactly for patriotic reasons, but rather by virtue of conflicts between imperialists — was Moise Tshombe, who initiated the secession of Katanga with Belgian support? And how can one justify, how can one explain, that at the end of all the UN activities there, Tshombe, dislodged from Katanga, should return as lord and master of the Congo? Who can deny the sad role that the imperialists compelled the United Nations to play?*

To sum up: dramatic mobilizations were carried out to avoid the secession of Katanga, but today Tshombe is in power, the wealth of the Congo is in imperialist hands — and the expenses have to be paid by the honorable nations. The merchants of war certainly do good business! That is why the government of Cuba supports the just stance of the Soviet Union in refusing to pay the expenses for this crime.

And as if this were not enough, we now have flung in our faces these latest acts that have filled the world with indignation. Who are the perpetrators? Belgian paratroopers, carried by US planes, who took off from British bases. We remember as if it

---

*   In mid-1964, a revolt broke out in the Congo led by followers of murdered Prime Minister Patrice Lumumba. In an effort to crush the uprising, during November US planes ferried Belgian troops and mercenaries to rebel-held territory. These forces carried out a massacre of thousands of Congolese. The year following his address to the United Nations, Che Guevara led a group of Cubans to assist the national liberation movement in the Congo.

were yesterday that we saw a small country in Europe, a civilized and industrious country, the Kingdom of Belgium, invaded by Hitler's hordes. We were embittered by the knowledge that this small nation was massacred by German imperialism, and we felt affection for its people. But this other side of the imperialist coin was the one that many of us did not see. Perhaps the sons of Belgian patriots who died defending their country's liberty are now murdering in cold blood thousands of Congolese in the name of the white race, just as they suffered under the German heel because their blood was not sufficiently Aryan.

Our liberated eyes open now on new horizons and can see what yesterday, in our condition as colonial slaves, we could not observe: that "Western Civilization" disguises behind its showy facade a picture of hyenas and jackals. That is the only name that can be applied to those who have gone to fulfill such "humanitarian" tasks in the Congo. A carnivorous animal that feeds on unarmed peoples. That is what imperialism does to men. That is what distinguishes the imperial "white man."

All free men and women of the world must be prepared to avenge the crime of the Congo. Perhaps many of those soldiers, who were turned into sub-humans by imperialist machinery, believe in good faith that they are defending the rights of a superior race. In this Assembly, however, those peoples whose skins are darkened by a different sun, colored by different pigments, constitute the majority. And they fully and clearly understand that the difference between human beings does not lie in the color of their skin, but in the forms of ownership of the means of production, in the relations of production.

[...]

We shall only touch on the questions of economic development and international trade that are broadly represented in the agenda. In this very year of 1964 the Geneva conference was held at which a multitude of matters related to these aspects of international relations were dealt with. The warnings and forecasts of our delegation were fully confirmed, to the misfortune of the economically dependent countries.

We wish only to point out that insofar as Cuba is concerned, the United States of America has not implemented the explicit recommendations of that conference, and recently the US government also prohibited the sale of medicines to Cuba. By doing so it divested itself, once and for all, of the mask of humanitarianism with which it attempted to disguise the aggressive nature of its blockade against the people of Cuba.

Furthermore, we state once more that the scars left by colonialism that impede the development of the peoples are expressed not only in political relations. The so-called deterioration of the terms of trade is nothing but the result of the unequal exchange between countries producing raw materials and industrial countries, which dominate markets and impose the illusory justice of equal exchange of values.

So long as the economically dependent peoples do not free themselves from the capitalist markets and, in a firm bloc with the socialist countries, impose new relations between the exploited and the exploiters, there will be no solid economic development. In certain cases there will be retrogression, in which the weak countries will fall under the political domination of the imperialists and colonialists.

Finally, distinguished delegates, it must be made clear that in the area of the Caribbean, maneuvers and preparations for aggression against Cuba are taking place, on the coasts of Nicaragua above all, in Costa Rica as well, in the Panama Canal Zone, on Vieques Island in Puerto Rico, in Florida and possibly in other parts of US territory and perhaps also in Honduras. In these places Cuban mercenaries are training, as well as mercenaries of other nationalities, with a purpose that cannot be the most peaceful one.

After a big scandal, the government of Costa Rica—it is said— has ordered the elimination of all training camps of Cuban exiles in that country. Nobody knows whether this position is sincere, or whether it is a simple alibi because the mercenaries training there were about to commit some misdeed. We hope that full cognizance will be taken of the real existence of bases for aggression, which we denounced long ago, and that the world will ponder the international responsibility of the government of a country that authorizes and facilitates the training of mercenaries to attack Cuba.

We should note that news of the training of mercenaries in different parts in the Caribbean and the participation of the US government in such acts is presented as completely natural in the newspapers in the United States. We know of no Latin American voice that has officially protested this. This shows the cynicism with which the US government moves its pawns.

The astute foreign ministers of the OAS had eyes to see Cuban emblems and to find "irrefutable" proof in the weapons that the Yankees exhibited in Venezuela, but they do not see the preparations for aggression in the United States, just as they did not hear the voice of President Kennedy, who explicitly declared himself the aggressor against Cuba at the Bay of Pigs [invasion of April 1961]. In some cases, it is a blindness provoked by the hatred against our revolution by the ruling classes of the Latin American countries. In others—and these are sadder and more deplorable— it is the product of the dazzling glitter of mammon.

As is well known, after the tremendous commotion of the so-called Caribbean [missile] crisis, the United States undertook certain commitments with the Soviet Union. These culminated in the withdrawal of certain types of weapons that the continued acts of aggression of the United States—such as the mercenary attack at the Bay of Pigs and threats of invasion against our homeland— had compelled us to install in Cuba as an act of legitimate and essential defense.

The United States, furthermore, tried to get the UN to inspect our territory. But we emphatically refuse, since Cuba does not recognize the right of the United States, or of anyone else in the world, to determine the type of weapons Cuba may have within its borders.

In this connection, we would abide only by multilateral agreements, with equal obligations for all the parties concerned. As Fidel Castro has said: "So long as the concept of sovereignty exists as the prerogative of nations and of independent peoples, as a right of all peoples, we will not accept the exclusion of our people from that right. So long as the world is governed by these principles, so long as the world is governed by those concepts that have universal validity because they are universally accepted and recognized by the peoples, we will not accept the attempt to deprive us of any of those rights, and we will renounce none of those rights."

The secretary-general of the United Nations, U Thant, understood our reasons. Nevertheless, the United States attempted to establish a new prerogative, an arbitrary and illegal one: that of violating the airspace of a small country. Thus, we see flying over our country U-2 aircraft and other types of spy planes that, with complete impunity, fly over our airspace. We have made all the necessary warnings for the violations of our airspace to cease, as well as for a halt to the provocations of the US Navy against our sentry posts in the zone of Guantánamo, the buzzing by aircraft of our ships or the ships of other nationalities in international waters, the pirate attacks against ships sailing under different flags, and the infiltration of spies, saboteurs and weapons onto our island.

We want to build socialism. We have declared that we are supporters of those who strive for peace. We have declared ourselves to be within the group of Nonaligned countries, although we are Marxist-Leninists, because the Nonaligned countries, like ourselves, fight imperialism. We want peace. We want to build a better life for our people. That is why we avoid, insofar as possible, falling into the provocations manufactured by the Yankees. But we know the mentality of those who govern them. They want to make us pay a very high price for that peace. We reply that the price cannot go beyond the bounds of dignity.

And Cuba reaffirms once again the right to maintain on its territory the weapons it deems appropriate, and its refusal to recognize the right of any power on earth — no matter how powerful — to violate our soil, our territorial waters, or our airspace.

If in any assembly Cuba assumes obligations of a collective nature, it will fulfill them to the letter. So long as this does not happen, Cuba maintains all its rights, just as any other nation. In the face of the demands of imperialism, our prime minister laid out the five points necessary for the existence of a secure peace in the Caribbean. They are:

1. A halt to the economic blockade and all economic and trade pressures by the United States, in all parts of the world, against our country.

2. A halt to all subversive activities, launching and landing of weapons and explosives by air and sea, organization of mercenary invasions, infiltration of spies and saboteurs, acts all carried out from the territory of the United States and some accomplice countries.

3. A halt to pirate attacks carried out from existing bases in the United States and Puerto Rico.

4. A halt to all the violations of our airspace and our territorial waters by US aircraft and warships.

5. Withdrawal from the Guantánamo naval base and return of the Cuban territory occupied by the United States."

None of these elementary demands has been met, and our forces are still being provoked from the naval base at Guantánamo. That base has become a nest of thieves and a launching pad for them into our territory. We would tire this Assembly were we to give a detailed account of the large number of provocations of all kinds. Suffice it to say that including the first days of December, the number amounts to 1,323 in 1964 alone. The list covers minor provocations such as violation of the boundary line, launching of objects from the territory controlled by the United States, the commission of acts of sexual exhibitionism by US personnel of both sexes, and verbal insults. It includes others that are more serious, such as shooting off small caliber weapons, aiming weapons at our territory, and offenses against our national flag. Extremely serious provocations include those of crossing the boundary line and starting fires in installations on the Cuban side, as well as rifle fire. There have been 78 rifle shots this year, with the sorrowful toll of one death: that of Ramón López Peña, a soldier, killed by two shots fired from the US post three and a half kilometers from the coast on the northern boundary. This extremely grave provocation took place at 7:07 p.m. on July 19, 1964, and the prime minister of our government publicly stated on July 26 that if the event were to recur he would give orders for our troops to repel the aggression. At the same time orders were given for the withdrawal of the forward line of Cuban forces to positions farther away from the boundary line and construction of the necessary fortified positions.

One thousand three hundred and twenty-three provocations in 340 days amount to approximately four per day. Only a perfectly disciplined army with a morale such as ours could resist so many hostile acts without losing its self-control.

Forty-seven countries meeting at the Second Conference of Heads of State or Government of Nonaligned Countries in Cairo unanimously agreed:

Noting with concern that foreign military bases are in practice a means of bringing pressure on nations and retarding their emancipation and development, based on their own ideological, political, economic and cultural ideas, the conference declares its unreserved support to the countries that are seeking to secure the elimination of foreign bases from their territory and calls upon all states maintaining troops and bases in other countries to remove them immediately.

The conference considers that the maintenance at Guantánamo (Cuba) of a military base of the United States of America, in defiance of the will of the government and people of Cuba and in defiance of the provisions embodied in the declaration of the Belgrade conference, constitutes a violation of Cuba's sovereignty and territorial integrity.

Noting that the Cuban government expresses its readiness to settle its dispute over the base at Guantánamo with the United States of America on an equal footing, the conference urges the US government to open negotiations with the Cuban government to evacuate their base.

The government of the United States has not responded to this request of the Cairo conference and is attempting to maintain indefinitely by force its occupation of a piece of our territory, from which it carries out acts of aggression such as those detailed earlier.

The Organization of American States — which the people also call the US Ministry of Colonies — condemned us "energetically," even though it had just excluded us from its midst, ordering its members to break off diplomatic and trade relations with Cuba. The OAS authorized aggression against our country at any time and under any pretext, violating the most fundamental international laws, completely disregarding the United Nations. Uruguay, Bolivia, Chile and Mexico opposed that measure, and the government of the United States of Mexico refused to comply with the sanctions that had been approved. Since then we have had no relations with any Latin American countries except Mexico, and this fulfills one of the necessary conditions for direct aggression by imperialism.

We want to make clear once again that our concern for Latin America is based on the ties that unite us: the language we speak, the culture we maintain, and the common master we had. We have no other reason for desiring the liberation of Latin America from the US colonial yoke. If any of the Latin American countries here decide to reestablish relations with Cuba, we would be willing to do so on the basis of equality, and without viewing that recognition of Cuba as a free country in the world to be a gift to our government. We won that recognition with our blood in the days of the liberation struggle. We acquired it with our blood in the defense of our shores against the Yankee invasion.

Although we reject any accusations against us of interference in the internal affairs of other countries, we cannot deny that we sympathize with those people who strive for their freedom. We must fulfill the obligation of our government and people to state clearly and categorically to the world that we morally support and stand in solidarity with peoples who struggle anywhere in the world to make a reality of the rights of full sovereignty proclaimed in the UN Charter.

It is the United States that intervenes. It has done so historically in Latin America. Since the end of the last century Cuba has experienced this truth, but so have Venezuela, Nicaragua, Central America in general, Mexico, Haiti, and the Dominican Republic. In recent years, apart from our people, Panama has experienced direct aggression, where the marines in the Canal Zone opened fire in cold blood against the defenseless people; the Dominican Republic, whose coast was violated by the Yankee fleet to avoid an outbreak of the just fury of the people after the death of [dictator of the Dominican Republic] Trujillo [in 1961]; and Colombia, whose capital was taken by assault as a result of a rebellion provoked by the assassination of [Colombian Liberal Party leader Eliécer] Gaitán [in 1948].

Covert interventions are carried out through military missions that participate in internal repression, organizing forces designed for that purpose in many countries, and also in coups d'état, which have been repeated so frequently on the Latin American continent during recent years. Concretely, US forces intervened in the repression of the peoples of Venezuela, Colombia and Guatemala, who fought with weapons for their freedom. In Venezuela, not only do US forces advise the army and the police, but they also direct acts of genocide carried out from the air against the peasant population in vast insurgent areas. And the Yankee companies operating there exert pressures of every kind to increase direct interference. The imperialists are preparing to repress the peoples of the Americas and are establishing an International of Crime.

The United States intervenes in Latin America invoking the defense of free institutions. The time will come when this Assembly will acquire greater maturity and demand of the US government guarantees for the lives of the blacks and Latin Americans who live in that country, most of them US citizens by origin or adoption.

Those who kill their own children and discriminate daily against them because of the color of their skin; those who let the murderers of blacks remain free, protecting them, and furthermore punishing the black population because they demand their legitimate rights as free human beings—how can those who do this consider themselves guardians of freedom? We understand that today the Assembly is not in a position to ask for explanations of these acts. It must be clearly established, however, that the government of the United States is not the champion of freedom, but rather the perpetrator of exploitation and oppression against the peoples of the world and against a large part of its own population.

To the ambiguous language with which some delegates have described the case of Cuba and the OAS, we reply with plain words and we proclaim that the peoples of Latin America will make those servile, sell-out governments pay for their treason.

Cuba, distinguished delegates, a free and sovereign state with no chains binding it to anyone, with no foreign investments on its territory, with no proconsuls directing its policy, can speak with its head held high in this Assembly and can demonstrate the justice of the phrase by which it has been baptized: "Free Territory of the Americas."

Our example will bear fruit in the continent, as it is already doing to a certain extent in Guatemala, Colombia and Venezuela.

There is no small enemy nor insignificant force, because no longer are there isolated peoples. As the Second Declaration of Havana states:

> No nation in Latin America is weak—because each forms part of a family of 200 million brothers, who suffer the same miseries, who harbor the same sentiments, who have the same enemy, who dream about the same better future, and who count upon the solidarity of all honest men and women throughout the world...
>
> This epic before us is going to be written by the hungry Indian masses, the peasants without land, the exploited workers. It is going to be written by the progressive masses, the honest and brilliant intellectuals, who so greatly abound in our suffering Latin American lands. Struggles of masses and ideas. An epic that will be carried forward by our peoples, mistreated and scorned by imperialism; our people, unreckoned with until today, who are now beginning to shake off their slumber. Imperialism considered us a weak and submissive flock; and now it begins to be terrified of that flock; a gigantic flock of 200 million Latin Americans in whom Yankee monopoly capitalism now sees its gravediggers...

But now from one end of the continent to the other they are signaling with clarity that the hour has come — the hour of their redemption. Now this anonymous mass, this America of color, somber, taciturn America, which all over the continent sings with the same sadness and disillusionment, now this mass is beginning to enter definitively into its own history, it is beginning to write its history with its own blood, it is beginning to suffer and die for that history.

Because now in the fields and mountains of the Americas, on its plains and in its jungles, in the wilderness and in the traffic of cities, on the banks of its great oceans or rivers, this world is beginning to tremble. Anxious hands are stretched forth, ready to die for what is theirs, to win those rights that were laughed at by one and all for 500 years. Yes, now history will have to take the poor of the Americas into account, the exploited and spurned of the Americas, who have decided to begin writing their history for themselves and for all time. Already they can be seen on the roads, on foot, day after day, in an endless march of hundreds of kilometers to the governmental "eminences," there to obtain their rights.

Already they can be seen armed with stones, sticks, machetes, in one direction and another, each day occupying lands, sinking hooks into the land that belongs to them and defending it with their lives. They can be seen carrying signs, slogans, flags, letting them fly in the mountain or prairie winds. And the wave of anger, of demands for justice, of claims for rights trampled underfoot, which is beginning to sweep the lands of Latin America, will not stop. That wave will swell with every passing day. For that wave is composed of the greatest number, the majorities in every respect, those whose labor amasses the wealth and turns the wheels of history. Now they are awakening from the long, brutalizing sleep to which they had been subjected,

For this great mass of humanity has said, "Enough!" and has begun to march. And this march of giants will not be halted until they conquer true independence—for which they have died in vain more than once. Today, however, those who die will die like the Cubans at the Bay of Pigs. They will die for their own true and never-to-be-surrendered independence.

All this, distinguished delegates, this new will of a whole continent, of Latin America, is made manifest in the cry proclaimed daily by our masses as the irrefutable expression of their decision to fight and to paralyze the armed hand of the invader. It is a cry that has the understanding and support of all the peoples of the world and especially of the socialist camp, headed by the Soviet Union.

That cry is: *Patria o muerte!* [Homeland or death!]

From: *Che Guevara Reader: Writings on Politics and Revolution* by Ernesto Che Guevara

From left to right: Che Guevara, Fidel Castro, Calixto García, Ramiro Valdés, and Juan Almeida in the Sierra Maestra.

Che Guevara during the revolutionary war in Cuba.

Che Guevara at El Hombrito in the Sierra Maestra.

Che Guevara and Camilo Cienfuegos.

Che Guevara in the Sierra Maestra.

Fidel Castro and Che Guevara in the Sierra Maestra.

Che Guevara (center) with members of Column No. 4 celebrating New Years 1958.

Fidel Castro showing Haydée Santamaría (left) and Celia Sánchez how to use a rifle.

From left to right: José Argudín, Che Guevara, Aleida March, Harry "Pombo" Villegas and Ramón Pardo Guerra in Santa Clara, December 1958.

The derailment of the armored train in Santa Clara, December 1958.

Che in Placetas, Las Villas, December 1958.

Aleida March and Che Guevara.

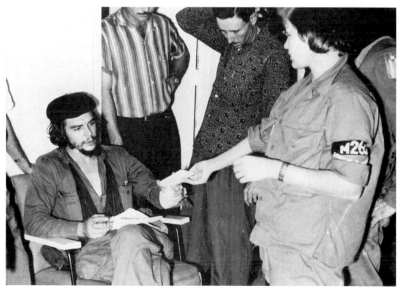

Before the surrender of Santa Clara, Che Guevara receives a message from Aleida March.

Che Guevara with Aleida March in Las Villas, December 1958.

Che Guevara and Aleida March on their wedding day, 1959. Raúl Castro and Vilma Espín are to the left.

Che Guevara and Aleida March with their four children, Havana, Cuba.

GUEVARA

Che Guevara addressing the UN General Assembly, New York, December 11, 1964.

Che Guevara during a CBS interview, New York, December 1964.

Interview with Lisa Howard, New York, December 1964.

Che Guevara addressing the UN General Assembly, New York, December 11, 1964.

Che Guevara as "Ramón Benítez" with Aleida March in one of their last photographs together.

Che Guevara in disguise with Fidel Castro before leaving Cuba.

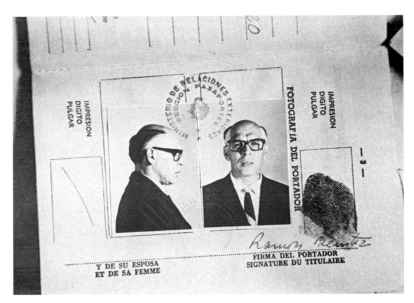

False passport in the name of Ramón Benítez used by Che Guevara to enter Bolivia secretly in 1966.

Self-portrait taken by Che Guevara in the Hotel Copacabana, La Paz, Bolivia, where he was undercover before joining the other guerrillas.

Tuma and Che Guevara (in disguise) on the way to the guerrilla camp in Bolivia.

From left to right: Arturo, Tuma, Che, Loro, and Pombo soon after Che's arrival at the guerrilla camp in Bolivia.

Che Guevara, Pombo, and Marcos.

Che Guevara on guard duty in the observation post, Bolivia, 1967.

Tania (Tamara Bunke) at the guerrilla camp in Bolivia.

From left to right: Inti, Pombo, Urbano, Rolando, Alejandro, Tuma, Arturo, and Moro.

From left to right: Urbano, Miguel, Che, Marcos, Chino, Pachungo, Pombo, Inti, and Loro.

Che Guevara in Bolivia.

Final entries in Che Guevara's Bolivian Diary, October 1967.

"WHEREVER DEATH MAY SURPRISE
US, LET IT BE WELCOME IF OUR
BATTLE CRY HAS REACHED EVEN ONE
RECEPTIVE EAR, IF ANOTHER HAND
REACHES OUT TO TAKE UP OUR ARMS,
AND OTHERS COME FORWARD TO
JOIN IN OUR FUNERAL DIRGE WITH
THE RATTLING OF MACHINE GUNS
AND WITH NEW CRIES OF STRUGGLE
AND VICTORY."

ERNESTO CHE GUEVARA

PART TWO

GUERRILLA

THE MOVIE "CHE" (PART 2)

IS BASED ON

THE BOLIVIAN DIARY

BY ERNESTO CHE GUEVARA

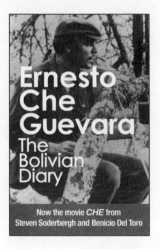

EXCERPTS OF THIS BOOK ARE REPRODUCED HERE

BOLIVIA

The following are extracts from *The Bolivian Diary* by Ernesto Che Guevara.

NOVEMBER 7, 1966

Today begins a new phase. We arrived at the [Ñacahuazú] farm at night. The trip went quite well. After we got to Cochabamba, conveniently disguised, Pachungo and I made some contacts and then traveled by jeep for two days, in two vehicles.

As we approached the farm, we stopped and continued in only one vehicle to avoid arousing the suspicion of the neighboring landowner, who is muttering that our business must be devoted to manufacturing cocaine. Oddly enough, the ineffable Tumaini is apparently identified as the chemist of our group. On discovering my identity on the way to the farm during the second trip, Bigotes almost drove into a ditch, leaving the jeep nearly hanging over it. We walked about 20 kilometers, reaching the farm after midnight, where there are three workers from the [Bolivian Communist] party.

Bigotes indicated he was ready to work with us, whatever the party does, but he is loyal to [leader of the Bolivian Communist Party Mario] Monje, whom he respects and seems to like.

According to him, Rodolfo is similarly disposed, as is Coco, but we should try to get the party to join the struggle. I asked him to help us and to refrain from mentioning anything to the party until the arrival of Monje, who is on a trip to Bulgaria; he agreed to both things.

ANALYSIS OF THE MONTH (NOVEMBER 1966)

Everything has gone quite well; my arrival was without incident; half the troops have arrived, also without incident, although they were somewhat delayed; Ricardo's main collaborators are joining the struggle, come what may. The general outlook seems good in this remote region and everything indicates that we could be here for practically as long as necessary. The plans are: to wait for the rest of the troops, increase the number of Bolivians to at least 20, and then commence operations. We still need to see how Monje reacts and how [Moisés] Guevara's people conduct themselves.

DECEMBER 31, 1966

At 7:30 El Médico [Ernesto] arrived with the news that Monje was there. I went to meet him with Inti, Tuma, Urbano, and Arturo. The reception was cordial, but tense; the obvious question, what are you here for? hung in the air. He was accompanied by Pan Divino, the new recruit, Tania [Tamara Bunke], who came to receive instructions, and Ricardo, who will now stay with us.

The conversation with Monje began with generalities but came down to his fundamental position, summarized by three basic conditions:

1) He will resign from the leadership of the party, but he will at least ensure it remains neutral and he will recruit cadres for the struggle.

2) He will head the political-military struggle for as long as the revolution is taking place in Bolivian territory.

3) He will handle relations with other South American parties, and try to convince them to support liberation movements. (He used Douglas Bravo [in Venezuela] as an example.)

I responded, saying that the first point was up to him, as secretary of the party, although I considered his position to be a grave error.

It was vacillating and compromising and protected those who should be condemned by history for abandoning their principles. Time will prove me right.

Concerning the third point, I had no objections to his attempting this, but it was doomed to fail. To ask Codovila to support Douglas Bravo was like asking him to condone an uprising in his own party. Time will be the judge here too.

On the second point, there was no way I could accept his proposal. I had to be military chief and would not accept any ambiguity on this. Here the discussion got stuck and went around and around in a vicious circle.

We left it that Monje would think it over and talk to his Bolivian compañeros. We moved on to the new camp and there he spoke with everyone, presenting the ultimatum that they could either stay or support the party; everyone opted to stay, which he seemed to take quite hard.

At 12:00, we made a toast, pointing out the historical importance of this date. I replied, taking advantage of his words and marking this moment as the new Cry of Murillo of the revolution on this continent, saying that our lives meant nothing when faced with the fact of the revolution.

Fidel sent me the attached messages.

ANALYSIS OF THE MONTH (DECEMBER 1966)

The team of Cubans has been successfully completed; morale is good and there are only minor problems. The Bolivians are doing well, although few in number. Monje's attitude can delay the development on the one hand, but on the other, can free me from political constraints. Apart from waiting for more Bolivians, the next steps are to speak with Guevara and with the Argentines Mauricio and Jozami (Masetti and the dissident party).

ANALYSIS OF THE MONTH (JANUARY 1967)

As I expected, Monje's position was at first evasive and then treacherous.

The party has taken up arms against us and I do not know where this will lead, but it will not stop us and maybe, in the end, it will be to our advantage (I am almost certain of this). The most honest and militant people will be with us, although they are going through a more or less severe crisis of conscience.

Up to now, Guevara has responded well; we will see how he and his people act in the future.

Tania departed, but the Argentines have shown no sign of life and neither has she. Now the real guerrilla phase begins and we will test the troops; time will tell what they can do and what the prospects for the Bolivian revolution are.

Of everything that was envisioned, the slowest has been the incorporation of Bolivian combatants.

FEBRUARY 26, 1967

I spoke with Marcos and Pacho in the morning, asking for an explanation, and I became convinced that Marcos had insulted and mistreated Pacho, and might have threatened him with the machete, but had not hit him. Pacho, for his part, is prone to insulting others and has an innate tendency to bravado, which has been demonstrated at other times.

I waited until everyone was assembled and talked about the importance of our effort to get to the Rosita River; I explained these kinds of deprivations were an introduction to what was in store for us and that because of an inability to adapt to our new circumstances some shameful incidents had arisen, such as had occurred between the two Cubans. I criticized Marcos for his attitude and made it clear to Pacho that another incident like the last would lead to his dishonorable discharge from the guerrilla force. Pacho had first refused to continue with the radio and then had returned without telling me about the incident, and later he had probably lied when he said Marcos had hit him.

I told the Bolivians that if anyone felt unable to continue, they should refrain from using deceitful methods to be discharged; they should come to me and then they could leave the guerrilla force in peace.

We continued walking, trying to reach the Río Grande and then follow its course; we made it and were able to walk along it for just over a kilometer, but then we had to climb away from it because we could not get past a rocky cliff. Benjamín had fallen behind, having difficulties with his backpack and was physically exhausted; when he caught up, I ordered him to continue, which he did for 50 meters; but then he lost the trail on the climb and went on to a ledge to locate it. When I ordered Urbano to help him find the way, he made a sudden movement and fell into the water. He did not know how to swim. The current was so strong he was dragged away as he tried to gain his footing; we ran to save him, but as we were taking off our clothes, he disappeared under the water. Rolando swam toward him and tried to dive under, but the current carried him away. After five minutes we gave up hope. He was a weak lad, not cut out for this at all, but he had a great determination to succeed. The test was beyond him, his physique did not match his will. Now we have had our baptism of death on the banks of the Río Grande, in such an absurd way. We camped at 5:00 in the afternoon without finding the Rosita. We ate the last ration of beans.

FEBRUARY 28, 1967

Partial rest day. After breakfast (tea) I gave a brief talk, analyzing the death of Benjamín and telling some stories from the Sierra Maestra. Then the scouts set off to explore: Miguel, Inti, and Loro went up the Rosita, with instructions to walk for three and a half hours, which was what I believed was required to reach the Abapocito River, but this was not the case because there was no path. They found no recent signs of life. Joaquín and Pedro climbed up to the woods ahead of us, but they saw nothing—no path, not even a trace of a path. Alejandro and Rubio crossed the river but did not find a path either, although their search was superficial. Marcos directed the construction of a raft, which, as soon as it was finished, was used to cross at a bend in the river into which the Rosita flows. Five men's backpacks were taken across, but they took Miguel's and left Benigno's, and did the opposite thing with the men themselves. To make matters worse, Benigno left his shoes behind.

The raft could not be recovered and the second one is not finished, so we will wait to cross tomorrow.

ANALYSIS OF THE MONTH (FEBRUARY 1967)

Although I have no news of what is happening at the camp, everything is going reasonably well, with some exceptions, fatal in one instance.

From the outside, there is no news of the two men who should have arrived to complete the group; the Frenchman [Regís Debray] should be in La Paz by now and should come to the camp any day. I have no news of the Argentines or Chino [a Peruvian]. Messages are being communicated well in both directions. The party's position remains vacillating and two-faced, to say the very least, although when I speak with the new delegation and hear the latest explanation, this will be clearer.

The march has been going well enough, although it has been seriously affected by the accident that cost Benjamín his life. The men are still weak and not all of the Bolivians are able to hold up; the last few days of hunger have dampened their enthusiasm, which was already obvious after the group was divided.

Of the Cubans, two of those with little experience, Pacho and Rubio, have not responded well. Alejandro has done extremely well; of the old timers, Marcos is a constant headache and Ricardo is not up to speed. The rest are doing well. The next phase will be combat, and that will be decisive.

MARCH 17, 1967

Another tragedy before our first test in combat. Joaquín turned up mid-morning; Miguel and Tuma had gone to find him, carrying large pieces of meat. It was a real odyssey: they said they could not control the raft and it was carried down the Ñacahuazú River until it struck a whirlpool and overturned several times. The final outcome was that several backpacks were lost, as was almost all the ammunition, six rifles, and one man: Carlos. Carlos was thrown into the whirlpool along with Braulio but they met different fates: Braulio made it to the bank and could see Carlos being dragged under, unable to resist. Joaquín had already reached the shore farther downstream, and did not see him being swept away. Up to now, Carlos was considered the best man of the Bolivians in the rear guard, for his seriousness, discipline, and enthusiasm.

The lost weapons are: a Brno, belonging to Braulio; two M-1s, (Carlos's and Pedro's); three Mausers, (Abel's, Eusebio's, and Polo's). Joaquín informed me that he had seen Rubio and El Médico [Ernesto] on the other side and had ordered them to build a little raft and to return. At 14:00 they showed up with a long tale about their trials and tribulations; they were naked and Rubio was barefoot. Their raft had broken apart in the first whirlpool; they made it to the bank almost at the same place that we had.

Our departure is set for early tomorrow and Joaquín will leave at midday. I hope to have more news tomorrow during the course of the day. The morale of Joaquín's troops seems good.

MARCH 21, 1967

I spent the day in talks and discussions with Chino, going over some points, and with the Frenchman, Pelao, and Tania. The Frenchman brought news we had already heard about Monje, Kolle, Simón Reyes, etc. He came to stay, but I asked him to go back and organize a support network in France, stopping first in Cuba, which coincides with his desire to get married and to have a child with his compañera. I must write letters to [Jean-Paul] Sartre and Bertrand Russell so they can organize international support for the Bolivian liberation movement. He should also talk to a friend who will organize all channels of support, fundamentally financial, medical, and electronic—the latter in the form of an electrical engineer and equipment.

Pelao, of course, is ready to receive my orders and I proposed to him that he act as a kind of a coordinator, working for now only with the groups led by Jozami, Gelman, and Stamponi, and sending me five men to begin training. He is to send my greetings to [Argentine writer] María Rosa Oliver and the old man [Che's father]. I will give him 500 pesos to send off and 1,000 to get around with. If they accept, they should begin exploratory activities in northern Argentina and send me a report.

Tania made her contacts and the people came, but, according to her, she had to drive them here in a jeep, and although she intended to stay only one day, things got complicated. Jozami could not stay the first time, and the second time no contact was made because Tania was here. She talked about Iván with considerable disdain—I do not know what is at the bottom of it all. We received Loyola's account balance up to February 9 ($1,500). (She also informed us she had left the leadership of the [Bolivian Communist Party] youth group.)

Two reports from Iván were received; one was of no interest, only containing information about a military school, with some photos attached, and the other reported on other matters, but also of no great importance.

The main thing is that he could not decode the written message (D. XIII). A report was received from Antonio (D. XII) where he tries to justify his position. We heard a radio broadcast in which a death was announced, followed by a retraction, which indicates that what Loro said was true.

MARCH 23, 1967

A day of military events. Pombo wanted to organize a *góndola* to get provisions, but I opposed it until we clarified the matter of Marcos's replacement. Just after 8:00, Coco rushed in to report that a section of the army had fallen into our ambush. At this point the outcome has been three 60-mm mortars, 16 Mausers, two BZs, three Uzis, one .30-caliber machine gun, two radios, boots, etc. There were seven dead, 14 healthy prisoners, and four wounded, but we could not secure any provisions. An operations plan was captured, which revealed a plan to advance from both directions along the Ñacahuazú, making contact mid-way. We rapidly moved our troops to one side, with Marcos, and almost the entire vanguard at the end of the path of operations, while the center group and part of the rear guard remained in defensive positions; Braulio set up an ambush at the end of the other path of operations. We will spend the night this way to see if tomorrow the famous Rangers turn up. Two prisoners—a major and a captain—talked like parrots.

We decoded the message sent with Chino. It describes Debray's trip, the sending of $60,000, Chino's requests, and explains why they had not written to Iván. I also received a communication from Sánchez, which reports on the possibilities for setting up Mito at various points.

MARCH 24, 1967

The total haul is the following: 16 Mausers, three mortars with 64 shells, two BZs, 2,000 Mauser rounds, three Uzis with two clips each, and one .30-caliber machine gun with two cartridge belts. There are seven dead and 14 prisoners, including four wounded. Marcos was sent to explore but did not come up with anything; but planes are bombing close to our house.

I sent Inti to speak with the prisoners for the last time and to set them free, taking all the clothes we can use, but the two officers were questioned separately and went off with their clothes. We told the major that they had until 12:00 on the 27th to remove the dead bodies and offered a truce for the entire area of Lagunillas if he stayed here, but he said that he was retiring from the army.

The captain said he had just rejoined the army a year ago at the request of people from the party and that he had a brother studying in Cuba; he gave us the names of two other officers who would be willing to collaborate. When the planes began bombing they got a terrible fright, and it also scared two of our men: Raúl and Wálter. The latter had also been cowardly in the ambush.

Marcos scouted the area but found nothing. Ñato and Coco went upstream with the *"resaca* group" [rejects, literally dregs] to carry supplies, but the men had to be brought back because they did not want to do the hike. They must be discharged.

ANALYSIS OF THE MONTH (MARCH 1967)

This month was full of events, but the general panorama is characterized as follows:

- The phase of consolidation and purging of the guerrilla force — fully completed.

- The phase of slow development with the incorporation of some Cuban elements, who do not seem bad, and Guevara's people, who are generally low level (two deserters, one "talking" prisoner, three cowards, and two quitters.)

- The initial phase of the struggle, characterized by a precise and spectacular blow [the March 23 ambush of Bolivian Army troops], but marked by gross indecision before and after the fact (the withdrawal of Marcos, Braulio's action).

The beginning of the enemy's counteroffensive, characterized to this point by:

a) a tendency to take measures to isolate us,

b) a clamor at a national and an international level,

c) total ineffectiveness, so far, and

d) mobilization of peasants.

Evidently, we will have to hit the road before I expected and move on, leaving a group to recover, saddled with the burden of four possible informers.

The situation is not good, but now begins a new testing phase for the guerrilla force that will be of great benefit once surpassed.

APRIL 4, 1967

Almost a total disaster. At 14:30, we reached a place where there were guard tracks and even a paratrooper's beret and remains of US [Army] individual food rations. I decided to take the first house by force *[illegible in the original]*, which we did at 18:30. Guaraní [indigenous] farmhands came out and told us that the army had about 150 men who had withdrawn yesterday, and that the owner of the house had left to take his livestock away. They were charged with making a meal of pork and yucca, while our men went to occupy the second house belonging to *[illegible in the original]*. Loro, Coco, Aniceto, and later Inti went to the second house accompanied by one of the peasants.

The couple was not there, but when they arrived, the young farmhand escaped in the confusion. In the end, we established that approximately one company of the Second Regiment (the Bolívar) had been there and had left this morning. They had instructions to go down through the Tiraboy ravine, but they chose to leave by another route, so we never ran into them. There are no soldiers in Gutiérrez, but they will return tomorrow, so it is best not to hang around.

In the first house we found military gear, such as plates, canteens, even bullets and equipment; we appropriated everything. After eating well, but not excessively, the rear guard set off at 3:00 and we departed at 3:30. The vanguard should have left when they finished eating their last rations. We ourselves got lost and left farther down from the ambush site, which caused confusion until daylight.

APRIL 10, 1967

Dawn broke and the morning passed without much happening as we prepared to leave the creek, removing all traces of our presence, and then crossing through Miguel's ravine toward Pirirenda-Gutiérrez. Negro arrived very agitated mid-morning to warn us that 15 soldiers were coming downstream. Inti had gone to notify Rolando at the ambush site. There was no other option but to wait and so that is what we did; I dispatched Tuma so he could report back to me. The first reports soon arrived, with unfortunate news. Rubio (Jesús Suárez Gayol) had been mortally wounded. His body was carried to our camp; he had been shot in the head.

This is what happened: The ambush was made up of eight men from the rear guard and a reinforcement of three from the vanguard; they were spread out on both sides of the river. When Inti went to inform them that 15 soldiers were coming, he passed Rubio and realized he was in a very bad position, being clearly visible from the river. The soldiers advanced taking few precautions, searching the riverbanks for tracks. They ran into Braulio or Pedro before falling into the ambush. The exchange lasted a few seconds, leaving one dead and three wounded, plus six prisoners. Later a low-ranking officer was hit and four others escaped. Next to another wounded man, they found Rubio dying. His Garand had jammed and a grenade was beside him with the pin released but without having exploded. The prisoner could not be interrogated because he was seriously wounded and died shortly afterward, as did the commanding officer.

From interrogating the prisoners, the following information was gained: These 15 men belong to the same company that was upriver at the Ñacahuazú; they had crossed through the canyon, collected the skeletons, and then had occupied the camp. According to the soldiers, they had not found anything, although the radio reports that photos and documents had been found there. The company consists of 100 men, of which 15 accompanied a group of journalists to our camp. This group had left to go on a scouting expedition and returned at 17:00. The largest forces are in Pincal, and there are about 30 soldiers in Lagunillas; the group that had gone along the Tiraboy had probably been withdrawn to Gutiérrez. They described their odyssey, being lost in the woods without water and how they had to be rescued. Expecting that more of them would come later, I resolved to keep the ambush in place, which Rolando had moved forward about 500 meters, but now it was reinforced by the entire vanguard. At first I had ordered them to withdraw, but then it seemed logical to leave it as it was. Around 17:00, came information that the army was advancing with a large number of troops. There was nothing to do but wait. I sent off Pombo to get a clear idea of the situation. Some isolated shots were heard for a short time and Pombo returned to say they had fallen into our ambush again and that several were killed and a major had been taken prisoner.

This time, events unfolded like this: The soldiers had advanced along the river, but they were spread out and did not take any real precautions and we took them completely by surprise. This time there were seven dead, five wounded, and a total of 22 prisoners.

The balance sheet is the following: (There are no details due to a lack of information).

APRIL 11, 1967

We began the transfer of all our gear in the morning and we buried Rubio in a small, shallow grave, given our lack of materials. Inti stayed with the rear guard to accompany the prisoners and to set them free, as well as to look for more scattered weapons. The only result of the search was two new prisoners and their Garands. We gave two copies of our [*Communiqué: To the Bolivian People*] No. 1 to the major, who promised to pass them on to the press. The casualties are now 10 dead, including two lieutenants; 30 prisoners (a major, some non-commissioned officers, and the rest privates); six wounded — one from the first attack and the others from the second.

They are under the command of the Fourth Division, but mixed with elements of several other regiments; there are Rangers, paratroopers, and soldiers from the local area who are just kids.

Not until the afternoon did we finish the transfer and find a cave in which to leave the gear, but it is still not properly prepared. During the last trip, two cows took fright and ran away, so now all we have left is a calf.

Just as we reached the new camp very early, we ran into Joaquín and Alejandro, who had come with all their people. From their information, we concluded that what the soldiers reported was only a figment of Eustaquio's imagination and that moving here was a waste of time.

The radio reported a "new and bloody encounter" and mentioned nine dead from the army and at least four "confirmed" dead on our side.

A Chilean journalist gave a detailed description of our camp and reported the discovery of a photo of me, without a beard and with a pipe. There will have to be an investigation into how this was obtained. There is no proof that the upper cave has been found, although there are some suggestions this might be the case.

APRIL 12, 1967

I brought all the combatants together at 6:30, except for the four from the reject group, to hold a small memorial for Rubio where I noted that the first blood spilled was Cuban. I mentioned I had observed a tendency in the vanguard to depreciate the Cubans, a tendency that surfaced yesterday when Camba commented that he had less and less confidence in the Cubans, after an incident with Ricardo. I made a new call for unity as the only possible way to develop our army, pointing out we had increased our firepower and gained combat experience, but our number has not increased; to the contrary, it has decreased in the last few days.

After storing all our booty in a cave prepared well by Ñato, we left at 14:00 at a slow pace. We were so slow that we barely advanced and had to sleep by a small water hole, although we had just set out.

Now the army admits to 11 dead; either they found another corpse or someone died of their wounds. I began a little course on Debray's book.

Part of a message has been decoded, but it does not seem very important.

APRIL 25, 1967

Bad day. At about 10:00 Pombo returned from the lookout warning us that 30 soldiers were advancing toward the little house. Antonio stayed at the observation post. While we were getting ready, Antonio arrived with the news that there were 60 soldiers and they were preparing to advance. The lookout proved to be inefficient in giving us sufficient warning. We decided to set up an improvised ambush along the access path to the camp; quickly, we chose a short stretch along the creek with a visibility of 50 meters. I positioned myself there with Urbano and Miguel, who had the automatic rifle. El Médico [Moro], Arturo, and Raúl occupied a position on the right to impede anyone trying to flee or to advance that way. Rolando, Pombo, Antonio, Ricardo, Julio, Pablito, Darío, Willy, Luis, and León occupied the lateral position on the other side of the creek to completely cover the flank. Inti stayed at the river bed to attack anyone looking for refuge there. Ñato and Eustaquio went to the lookout with instructions to withdraw when the firing started. Chino remained behind, guarding the camp. My already meager troops were reduced by three men: Pacho, lost, with Tuma and Luis off looking for him.

In a while the army's advance guard appeared, which to our surprise included three German shepherds and their trainer. The animals were restless, but it did not seem that they had detected us. However, they continued to advance and I shot at the first dog, but missed. When I aimed at the guide, the M-2 jammed. Miguel killed the other dog, from what we could see, but it was not confirmed. No one else entered the ambush. Intermittent gunfire commenced at the army's flank. When the shooting was over, I sent Urbano to order a retreat, but he came back with the news that Rolando was wounded. Shortly, they brought him back, but he was already dying; he died as we began to give him plasma. A bullet had split his femur and all the surrounding nerves and vessels; he bled to death before we could do anything. We have lost the best man of the guerrilla force, one of its pillars, my compañero since he was basically a child, when he became the messenger for Column 4 [during the Cuban revolutionary war], through the invasion, and now to this new revolutionary venture. Of his sorrowful death, only one thing can be said, for a hypothetical future yet to materialize: "Thy brave little captain's corpse has stretched to immensity in its metallic form."

The rest of the day was spent on a slow withdrawal operation, collecting everything and the body of Rolando (Captain San Luis). Pacho joined us later: he had made a mistake and went to where Coco was, and it took him all night to return. At 3:00 we buried the body under a thin layer of earth. Benigno and Aniceto arrived at 16:00, reporting that they had fallen into an army ambush (or rather a skirmish), losing the backpacks but getting out unharmed. According to Benigno's calculations, this occurred as they had nearly reached the Ñacahuazú. Now we have the two natural exits blocked, so we will have to "head for the hills"; leaving along the Río Grande is not smart because it is predictable and would take us further from Joaquín, from whom we have had no news. At night we reached a crossroads: one leading to the Ñacahuazú and the other to the Río Grande, and we slept there; we will wait here for Coco and Camba to reunite our small troop. The balance sheet of the operation is extremely negative: Rolando was killed, but not only that—the losses we inflicted on the army cannot be more than two and a dog, even with everyone shooting, our position was not studied or prepared properly and those shooting could not see the enemy; and finally, the lookout system was very bad, failing to give us enough advance warning.

A helicopter landed twice at the priest's house; we do not know if it went to pick up the wounded, and aircraft bombed our previous positions, which indicates they have not advanced at all.

SUMMARY OF THE MONTH (APRIL 1967)

Things are developing normally, although we have to acknowledge two severe losses: Rubio and Rolando; the death of the latter is a severe blow because I was planning to give him command of an eventual second front. We have seen action four more times, all of them with generally positive results and one very good one—the ambush in which Rubio died.

On another level, we are totally cut off; illness has undermined the health of some compañeros, obliging us to divide our forces, which has greatly reduced our effectiveness; we have still not made contact with Joaquín; the peasant support base has yet to develop, although, it appears that the systematic terror they suffer will ensure the neutrality of most—support will come later. There has not been a single new recruit, and apart from the deaths, we have lost Loro, who disappeared after the action at Taperillas.

Of the points on military strategy noted above, we can emphasize:

a) The measures taken to control us have not been very effective to date, and while they bother us, they allow us some movement, given the army's weakness and lack of mobility; besides, after the last ambush against the dogs and the trainer, we can presume they will be more careful when entering the woods.

b) The clamor continues, but now from both sides; after the publication of my article in Havana ["Message to the Tricontinental"], there can be no doubt about my presence here.

It seems certain that the North Americans will intervene heavily here, having already sent helicopters and apparently the Green Berets, although they have not been seen around here.

c) The army (at least one or two companies) has improved its technique; they surprised us at Taperillas and were not demoralized at El Mesón.

d) The mobilization of peasants is nonexistent, except as informers, which is somewhat troublesome; but they are neither quick nor efficient, and of no consequence.

Chino's status has changed and he will be a combatant until the second or third front is established. Dantón and Carlos were victims of their own haste, almost desperation, to leave and of my lack of energy to stop them; now communication with Cuba is cut off (Dantón) and the plan of action for Argentina (Carlos) is lost.

In summary: A month in which all has developed normally, considering the inevitable contingencies of a guerrilla force. Morale is good among all the combatants who have had their preliminary test as guerrilla fighters.

MAY 8, 1967

From early in the morning I insisted that we organize the cave, retrieve the other can of lard, and refill the bottles, because that is all we have left to eat. At about 10:30, a few isolated shots were heard coming from the ambush site; two unarmed soldiers had come up the Ñacahuazú. Thinking it was an advance party, Pacho wounded one in the leg and the other superficially in the stomach. He said he had fired because they had not stopped at his command, but they, of course, had heard nothing.

The ambush was poorly coordinated and Pacho's actions were not good; he was very nervous. The situation was improved by sending Antonio and some others to the right side. The soldiers stated they were based near the Iquira, but in reality they were lying. At 12:00, two soldiers were captured as they came rushing down the Ñacahuazú, saying they were in a hurry because they had gone hunting and were following the Iquira to get back, when they discovered that their company had disappeared, so they went to find them; they were lying too. In fact, they are camped at the hunting field and they went off to look for food at our farm because the helicopter had not come to bring them supplies. The two we had captured were loaded with toasted and raw corn, four cans of onions, plus sugar and coffee, so today's problem was resolved, with the help of the lard, and we all ate great quantities, making some people sick.

Later, the sentries reported that the soldiers were continually scouting the area, going back and forth to the edge of river. Everyone was tense until the soldiers arrived, apparently 27 of them. They had noticed something unusual and the group advanced under the command of Second Lieutenant Laredo, who opened fire and fell dead on the spot, along with two recruits. Night had already fallen and our troops advanced, capturing six soldiers; the rest retreated.

The total result rashly speaking is three dead and 10 prisoners, two of them wounded; seven M-1s and four Mausers, personal gear, ammunition, and some food we consumed with the lard to mitigate our hunger. We slept there.

MAY 9, 1967

We got up at 4:00 (I never slept) and set the soldiers free, after giving them a lecture. We took their shoes, exchanged clothes with them, and sent the liars off in their underwear. They went toward the little farm, carrying their wounded. By 6:30 we completed our withdrawal toward Monos [Monkey] Creek along the path to the cave where we stored the captured goods.

The only food we have left is lard; I felt faint and had to sleep two hours to be able to continue at even this slow and halting pace; in general, the march has been that way. We ate soup made from the lard at the first water hole. The troops are sick and now many have edema. At night, the army reported on the action, naming its dead and wounded, but not its prisoners, and announcing major battles with heavy losses on our side.

SUMMARY OF THE MONTH (MAY 1967)

The negative point is the impossibility of making contact with Joaquín, in spite of our pilgrimage on the mountain range. There are indications he has moved to the north.

From a military viewpoint, we had three new battles with losses for the army and none for us. This, along with our forays into Pirirenda and Caraguatarenda, indicate success. The dogs have been declared ineffective and have been withdrawn from circulation.

The most important features are:

1) A total loss of contact with Manila [Havana], La Paz, and Joaquín, which reduces the number of our group to 25.

2) A complete failure to recruit peasants, although they are losing their fear of us and we are gaining their admiration. It is a slow and patient task.

3) The party, through Kolle, offers its collaboration, apparently without reservation.

4) The clamor surrounding Debray's case has given more momentum to our movement than 10 victories in battle could have.

5) The morale of the guerrilla movement is growing stronger and, if handled well, will certainly guarantee success.

6) The army remains disorganized and its technique has not significantly improved.

News of the month: The arrest and escape of Loro, who now should be rejoining us or heading to La Paz to make contact.

The army reported the arrest of all the peasants who collaborated with us in the Masicuri area; now comes the stage in which the peasants will be afraid of both sides, although in different ways; our triumph will signify the qualitative change necessary for their leap in development.

JUNE 14, 1967

[Che's youngest daughter] Celita: 4?

We spent the day by the "Aguada Fría" [Icy Water Hole] beside a fire, waiting for news from Miguel and Urbano, who were slashing a trail. The time set for moving out was 15:00, but Urbano arrived after that time to tell us they had reached a creek and had seen fences, and thought it might lead to the Río Grande. We stayed put eating the last of the stew; nothing else is left except for one ration of peanuts and three of *mote*.

I turned 39 [today] and am inevitably approaching the age when I need to consider my future as a guerrilla, but for now I am still "in one piece."

JUNE 26, 1967

A bad day for me. Everything seemed to be going smoothly, and I had sent five men to relieve those in the ambush along the road to Florida when shots were heard. We went there quickly on horseback and found a strange spectacle: amid total silence, the bodies of four young soldiers were lying in the sun on the sand by the river. We could not take their weapons because we did not know where the enemy was; it was 17:00 and we waited for nightfall to recover their weapons; Miguel sent word that he heard sounds of breaking branches to our left; Antonio and Pacho went to see, but I gave the order not to shoot if they saw nothing. Almost immediately shooting was heard all around and I ordered a retreat, as we were at a disadvantage under those conditions. The withdrawal was delayed and we got news of two wounded: Pombo in his leg and Tuma in his abdomen. We carried them quickly to the house to operate on them the best we could. Pombo's wound is superficial and will just cause headaches because of his lack of mobility. Tuma's wound destroyed his liver and produced intestinal perforations; he died during the operation. With his death, I have lost an inseparable compañero of recent years, one whose loyalty was unwavering and whose absence I feel now almost as if he were my own son. As he died, he asked that his watch be given to me, but this was not done immediately as they were busy tending to him; so he took it off himself and gave it to Arturo. The gesture revealed his wish that it be given to his son whom he had never met, as I had done before with the watches of fallen compañeros. I will wear it for the rest of the war. We loaded his body onto an animal and we will take it to be buried away from here.

We have taken prisoner two new spies: a *carabinero* lieutenant and a *carabinero*. They were lectured and set free wearing only their underwear, due to a misinterpretation of my orders, which were to take everything from them that we could use. We left with nine horses.

ANALYSIS OF THE MONTH (JUNE 1967)

The negative points are the impossibility of making contact with Joaquín and the gradual loss of men, each of which constitutes a serious defeat, although the army does not know this. We have had two skirmishes this month, causing the army four dead and three wounded, according to their own information.

The most important features are:

1) Continued total lack of contact, which reduces us now to 24 men, with Pombo wounded and with reduced mobility.

2) Continued lack of peasant recruitment. It is a vicious circle: to recruit we need to maintain constant activity in populated territory, and to do this we need more people.

3) The legend of the guerrilla force is growing like wildfire, now we are invincible superhumans.

4) The lack of contact extends to the party, although we have made an attempt through Paulino that could bring results.

5) Debray is still in the news but now he is linked with my case, and I have been identified the leader of the movement. We will see the result of this move by the government and if it is positive or negative for us.

6) The morale of the guerrilla fighters continues to be strong and their commitment to the struggle is increasing. All the Cubans are exemplary in combat and there are only two or three weak Bolivians.

7) The army continues to be useless in its military tactics, but is doing work among the peasants that we cannot ignore, transforming all members of the community into informers, either through fear or by fooling them about our goals.

8) The [June 23-24] massacre in the Siglo XX mines greatly im
   proves our outlook; if we can get our statement circulated, it
   will be a great clarifying factor.

Our most urgent task is to reestablish contact with La Paz, to
replenish our military and medical supplies, and to recruit 50 to
100 men from the city, even if the number of active combatants
comes to only 10 or 25.

JULY 5, 1967

Throughout the entire area, families with their belongings are
fleeing to escape the army's repression. We walked mingling with
oxen, pigs, chickens, and people until we reached Lagunillas;
where we left the Piojera River behind and followed its tributary,
the Lagunillas, for a kilometer. Serving as our guide was an
unhappy peasant called Ramón, whose family is stricken with the
proverbial fear found in this area. We slept beside the road; along
the way we met up with one of Sandoval Morón's uncles, who
lives in San Luis and seems much more alert.

JULY 30, 1967

I was really bothered by asthma and was awake all night. At 4:30,
when Moro was making coffee, he warned us that he had seen a
lantern coming across the river. Miguel, who was awake because
of the sentry change, went off with Moro to detain the travelers.
From the kitchen, I heard this exchange: "Hey, who goes there?"

"The Trinidad Detachment." Shooting broke out right away.
Immediately, Miguel brought back an M-1 and a cartridge belt
taken from a wounded soldier, along with the news that there

were 21 men on the road to Abapó and in Moroco there were 150. More casualties were inflicted on the enemy, but we could not be sure of the number in the prevailing confusion. It took a long time to load the horses and the black one got lost, and with it an ax and a mortar that had been taken from the enemy. It was already close to 6:00 and we lost even more time because some of the loads fell off. The end result was that the last of us to cross came under fire from the young soldiers who were becoming bolder. Paulino's sister was at her farm and received us very calmly, reporting that all the men in Moroco had been arrested and were in La Paz.

I hurried our troops along and went with Pombo, under fire again, past the river canyon where the path ends to where we could organize the resistance. I sent Miguel with Coco and Julio to take the forward position while I spurred on the cavalry. Covering the retreat were seven men from the vanguard, four from the rear guard, and Ricardo, who stayed behind to reinforce the defense. Benigno, (with Darío, Pablo, and Camba), was on the right side; the rest came along the left.

I had just given the order to rest at the first suitable spot, when Camba arrived with the news that Ricardo and Aniceto had been hit while crossing the river; I dispatched Urbano with Ñato and León and two horses, and sent for Miguel and Julio, leaving Coco at the forward post. They went through without receiving my instructions and, in a while, Camba returned again reporting that they and Miguel and Julio had been surprised and that the soldiers had advanced farther along. Miguel had withdrawn and was awaiting instructions. I sent Camba back again with Eustaquio, which left only Inti, Pombo, Chino, and me. At 13:00, I sent for Miguel, leaving Julio at the forward post and I withdrew with the group of men and horses. When I reached Coco's post on the high ground, the news caught up with me that all the survivors were there, that Raúl was dead, and that Ricardo and Pacho were wounded. Things happened like this: Ricardo and Aniceto were imprudently crossing the clearing when Ricardo was wounded. Antonio organized a line of fire between Arturo, Aniceto, and Pacho, and they rescued him, but then Pacho was wounded and a bullet to the mouth killed Raúl.

The withdrawal was difficult, dragging the two wounded men and with little help from Willy and Chapaco, especially the latter. Later Urbano and his group with the horses and Benigno and his people joined them. This left the other flank unguarded, through which the soldiers advanced and surprised Miguel. After a painful march through the woods, they came to the river and joined us. Pacho came on horseback but Ricardo could not ride and they had to carry him in a hammock. I sent Miguel, with Pablito, Darío, Coco, and Aniceto, to occupy the mouth of the first creek to the right, while we tended the wounded. Pacho had a superficial wound that went through his buttocks and the skin of his testicles, but Ricardo was in critical condition and the last plasma had been lost in Willy's backpack. Ricardo died at 22:00 and we buried him near the river, in a well-hidden place so that the soldiers could not find him.

JULY 31, 1967

At 4:00 we set off along the river, and after taking a shortcut, headed downriver without leaving tracks; later in the morning we reached the creek where Miguel had set up the ambush, but he had misunderstood the order and had left tracks. We walked upstream some four kilometers and went deep into the woods, covering our tracks and camping close to one of the creek's tributaries. At night I went through the errors of the action:

1) bad location of the campsite;

2) poor use of time, which enabled them to shoot at us;

3) an excess of confidence, which caused the loss of Ricardo and then of Raúl during the rescue; and

4) lack of decisiveness in saving all the gear.

We lost 11 backpacks with medicines, binoculars, and some potentially damaging items, such as the tape recorder onto which we copied the messages from Manila, Debray's book with my notes in it, and a book by Trotsky; all this does not take into account the political value that this haul has for the government and the confidence it will give the soldiers. We estimate about two dead and up to five wounded on their side, but there are two contradictory news reports: one, from the army, acknowledges four dead and four wounded on the 28th, and another from Chile talks of six wounded and three dead on the 30th. The army later issued another statement announcing they had found a body and that the second lieutenant was out of danger. Of our dead, it is hard to say how to categorize Raúl, given his introspection; he was not much in combat or at work, but he was always interested in political problems, although he never asked any questions. Ricardo was the most undisciplined of the Cuban group and the least resolute facing daily sacrifices, but he was an extraordinary combatant and an old comrade in arms from the first failure of Segundo [Jorge Ricardo Masetti], in the Congo, and now here. It is another tangible loss, due to his capabilities. We are now 22 men, with two wounded, (Pacho and Pombo), and me, with full-blown asthma.

ANALYSIS OF THE MONTH (JULY 1967)

We still have the same negative points as the previous month, namely: the impossibility of contact with Joaquín and the outside world, and the loss of men. Now we have 22 men, with three disabled (including me), which decreases our mobility. We have had three encounters, including the taking of Samaipata, causing the army about 7 dead and 10 wounded, approximate figures from conflicting reports. We have lost two men and have one wounded.

The most important features are:

1) Total loss of contact continues.

2) Continued sense of the lack of peasant recruitment, although there are some encouraging signs in the reception from peasants whom we have known for a while.

3) The legend of the guerrilla force is acquiring continental dimensions; [Argentine President] Onganía is closing the borders and Peru is taking precautions.

4) The attempt at contact through Paulino failed.

5) The morale and combat experience of the guerrilla fighters is increasing with each battle; Camba and Chapaco remain the weak ones.

6) The army continues to be ineffective, but there are units that appear to be more combative.

7) The political crisis of the government is growing, but the United States is giving small loans, which are of great assistance in tempering the level of Bolivian discontent.

The most urgent tasks are: To reestablish contact, to recruit combatants, and to obtain medicines.

AUGUST 8, 1967

We walked for something like an hour, but to me it seemed like two because of the exhaustion of the little mare; at one point, I slashed her neck, opening a deep wound. The new campsite is probably the last one with water until we reach the Rosita or the Río Grande; the *macheteros* are 40 minutes from here (two to three kilometers). I appointed a group of eight men for the following mission: They will leave from here tomorrow, and hike all day; the next day, Camba is to return and report; the day after, Pablito and Darío will return with the news from that day; the other five will proceed to Vargas's house and from there Coco and Aniceto will return to report on how things are going. Benigno, Julio, and Ñato will continue on to the Ñacahuazú to get the medicine for me. They should go very carefully to avoid ambushes; we will proceed and meet either at Vargas's house, depending on our speed, or farther up at the creek that runs in front of the cave on the Río Grande, the Masicuri (Honorato), or the Ñacahuazú. There is news from the army saying that an arms cache was discovered in one of our camps.

I gathered everyone together tonight to make the following speech: We are in a difficult situation; Pacho is recuperating, but I am a complete wreck and the incident with the little mare shows that at times I am beginning to lose control; this will be corrected, but we are all in this together and anyone who does not feel up to it should say so. This is one of those moments when great decisions have to be made; this type of struggle gives us the opportunity to become revolutionaries, the highest form of the human species, and it also allows us to emerge fully as men; those who are unable to achieve either of those two states should say so now and abandon the struggle. All the Cubans and some of the Bolivians committed themselves to stay until the end and so did Eustaquio, but he criticized Muganga for putting his backpack on the mule and for not carrying firewood, which provoked an angry response from Muganga. Julio lashed out at Moro and Pacho for similar reasons, which brought another angry response, this time from Pacho. I closed the discussion saying we were debating two things of a very different nature: one was if they were willing to continue or not, and the other was about petty arguments and internal problems of the guerrilla force which detract from the magnitude of the more important decision. I did not like the comments made by Eustaquio and Julio, but neither did I like the response from Moro and Pacho. In short, we have to be more revolutionary and strive to set an example.

AUGUST 29, 1967

A heavy and quite distressing day. The *macheteros* made very little progress and at one point went the wrong way, thinking they were going to the Masicuri. We set up camp at 1,600 meters, in a relatively humid place where a cane plant grows whose pulp quenches thirst. Some compañeros, Chapaco, Eustaquio, and Chino, are collapsing from lack of water. Tomorrow we have to head straight to wherever we can find water. The mules are holding up quite well.

There is no major news on the radio; the most important item is Debray's trial, which is being extended from one week to the next.

SUMMARY OF THE MONTH (AUGUST 1967)

Without doubt, this was the worst month we have had in this war. The loss of all the caves with the documents and medicines was a heavy blow, psychologically above all else. The loss of two men at the end of last month and the subsequent march on only horsemeat demoralized the troops and sparked the first case of desertion (Camba), which would otherwise constitute a net gain, but not under these circumstances. The lack of contact with the outside and with Joaquín, and the fact that the prisoners taken from his group talked, also demoralized the troops somewhat. My illness sowed uncertainty among several others and all this was reflected in our only clash, one in which we should have inflicted several enemy casualties, but only succeeded in wounding one of them. Besides this, the difficult march through the hills without water exposed some negative traits among the troops.

The most important features are:

1) We continue without contact of any kind and have no reasonable hope of establishing it in the near future.

2) We continue being unable to recruit peasants, which is logical considering how few dealings we have had with them recently.

3) There is a decline in combat morale; temporary, I hope.

4) The army has not increased its effectiveness or its aggressiveness.

We are at a low point in our morale and in our revolutionary reputation. The most urgent tasks are the same as last month, notably: to reestablish contact, to recruit combatants, and to obtain medicine and supplies.

It must be recognized that [Bolivians] Inti and Coco are becoming more and more outstanding as revolutionary and military cadres.

SEPTEMBER 7, 1967

A short trip. Only one ford was crossed and then we ran into difficulties with a rocky cliff; Miguel decided to set up camp to wait for us. Tomorrow we will conduct some good scouting expeditions. This situation is this: Aircraft are not looking for us here, despite having found the camp and the radio reports that I am the leader of the group. The question is: Are they afraid? Not likely. Do they consider it impossible to climb to the top? Based on what we have already done, of which they are aware, I do not think so. Do they want to let us advance to wait for us at some strategic point? It is possible. Do they think that we will stay in the Masicuri area for supplies? This is also possible. El Médico is much better, but I had a relapse and spent a sleepless night.

The radio brings news of the valuable information supplied by José Carrillo (Paco). We should make an example of him.

Debray responded to the accusations Paco made against him, saying that he likes to hunt and that is why he might have been seen with a rifle. Radio Cruz del Sur announced the discovery of the body of Tania the guerrilla on the banks of the Río Grande; it is news that does not ring true, like the news of Negro did; her body was taken to Santa Cruz, according to this radio station — and only this one, not the Altiplano station.

Altitude = 720 meters.

I spoke with Julio; he is doing very well but he is worried about the lack of contact and recruitment.

SEPTEMBER 8, 1967

A quiet day. We set up ambushes with eight men from morning to night, with Antonio and Pombo in charge. The animals are doing well, eating from the *chuchial*[3] and the mule is recovering from its injuries. Aniceto and Chapaco went to explore upriver and returned to say that the way was relatively good for the animals. Coco and Camba crossed the river with water up to their chests and climbed the hill in front of us, but they came back with little new information. I dispatched Miguel and Aniceto and the result of their more extensive exploration was that, according to

Miguel, it would be very difficult for the animals to get through. Tomorrow we will stay on this side, because there is always the possibility that the animals can get across the water with no loads on them.

The radio brought information that [Bolivian President] Barrientos attended the interment of the remains of Tania the guerrilla, who was given a "Christian burial." Later he was in Puerto Mauricio, where Honorato's house is; he made a proposal to those deceived Bolivians, who had never received their promised salaries that they should present themselves with their hands on their heads at army posts and no action would be taken against them. A small plane bombed the area below Honorato's house, as if making a show for Barrientos.

A Budapest daily is criticizing Che Guevara, a pathetic and apparently irresponsible figure, and applauds the Marxist stand of the Chilean [Communist] Party for taking a pragmatic position when faced with reality. How I would like to have power, for nothing more than to expose cowards and lackeys of all stripes and to rub their snouts in their own filth.

SEPTEMBER 26, 1967

Defeat. At the crack of dawn we came to Picacho where everyone was involved in a fiesta; this is the highest point we have reached: 2,280 meters; the peasants treated us very well and we carried on without too many fears, despite [General] Ovando having made assurances of my capture any moment now.

On reaching La Higuera, everything changed; the men had disappeared and only a few women remained. Coco went to the telegraph operator's house, where there is a telephone, and brought back a cable dated the 22nd, from which we learned that a sub-prefect of Vallegrande told the magistrate that if he had news of a guerrilla presence in the area, that information should be communicated to Vallegrande, which will cover the costs; the man had fled, but his wife assured us that he had not spoken to anyone today because everyone was off celebrating in the next town, Jagüey.

The vanguard set out at 13:00 to try to reach Jagüey and make a decision there about the mules and about El Médico; a little later I was talking to the only man left in town, who was very scared, when a coca merchant turned up, saying he had come from Vallegrande and Pucará and had seen nothing. He also was very nervous, which I attributed to our presence and let both of them go, in spite of the lies they told us. As I was going up to the crest of the hill, at approximately 13:30, shots coming from along the ridge indicated our men had fallen into an ambush. I organized the defense in the little village, to wait for the survivors, and set up an exit on the road that leads to the Río Grande. A few moments later, Benigno arrived, wounded, followed by Aniceto and Pablito, with a foot in a bad way. Miguel, Coco, and Julio had been killed and Camba had disappeared, leaving behind his backpack. The rear guard advanced quickly along the road and I followed them, bringing the two mules. Those in the rear were under fire and fell behind and Inti lost contact. After waiting for him for half an hour in an ambush position, with more gunfire coming from the hill, we decided to get out; but he caught up with us shortly. By this time we realized León had disappeared, and Inti said that he had seen his backpack by the gorge he came through; we saw a man who was walking fast along a canyon and concluded it was him. To try to throw them off our trail, we let the mules go in the canyon below and we proceeded along a small gorge that farther up had brackish water; we slept at 12:00 as it was impossible to go on.

SEPTEMBER 30, 1967

Another day of tension. In the morning, Radio Balmaseda of Chile announced that highly placed sources in the army announced Che Guevara is cornered in a canyon in the jungle. The local stations are silent; this could be a betrayal and they are convinced about our presence in the area. In a while, the soldiers began moving back and forth. At 12:00, 40 soldiers went past in separate columns with their weapons at the ready, on their way to the little house where they set up camp and established a lookout with nervous guards.

Aniceto and Pacho reported this. Inti and Willy returned with the news that the Río Grande was about two kilometers away, as the crow flies, and that there are three houses above the canyon, and that there are places to camp where we would be hidden from every side. We went to find water, and at 22:00 we began an exhausting night march, slowed down by Chino who walks very badly in the dark. Benigno is fine, but El Médico has not fully recovered.

SUMMARY OF THE MONTH (SEPTEMBER 1967)

It should have been a month of recuperation, and almost was, but the ambush in which Miguel, Coco, and Julio were killed ruined everything, and left us in a perilous position, losing León as well; losing Camba is a net gain.

We have had several small skirmishes: one in which we killed a horse; another in which we killed one soldier and wounded another; one where Urbano had a shoot-out with a patrol; and the disastrous ambush at La Higuera. Now we have abandoned the mules and I believe it will be a long time before we have animals like that again, unless I fall into another bad state of asthma.

On the other hand, there may be truth to the various reports about fatalities in the other [Joaquín's] group, so we must consider them wiped out, although it is still possible there is a small group wandering around, avoiding contact with the army, because the news of the death of seven people at once might well be false, or at least, exaggerated.

The features are the same as last month, except that now the army is demonstrating more effectiveness in action and the peasant masses are not helping us with anything and are becoming informers.

The most important task is to escape and seek more favorable areas; then focus on contacts, despite the fact that our urban network in La Paz is in a shambles, where we have also been hit hard. The morale of the rest of the troops has remained fairly high, and I only have doubts about Willy, who might take advantage of some commotion to escape, if he is not spoken to first.

OCTOBER 7, 1967

The 11-month anniversary of our establishment as a guerrilla force passed in a bucolic mood, with no complications, until 12:30 when an old woman tending her goats entered the canyon where we had camped and we had to take her prisoner. The woman gave us no reliable information about the soldiers, saying that she knew nothing because it had been a while since she had been over there. She only gave us information about trails, from which we conclude we are approximately one league from La Higuera, another from Jagüey, and about two more from Pucará. At 17:30, Inti, Aniceto, and Pablito went to the old woman's house; she has one daughter who is bedridden and the other is almost a dwarf. They gave her 50 pesos with instructions to not say a word, but we have little hope she will stick to her promise.[2]

The 17 of us set out under a slither of a moon; the march was exhausting and we left tracks in the canyon we walked through; there were no nearby houses, but there were potato seedbeds irrigated by ditches from the same creek. We stopped to rest at 2:00 because it was futile to continue. Chino becomes a real burden when we have to walk at night.

The army issued an odd report about the presence of 250 men in Serrano to block the escape of the 37 [guerrillas] that are said to be surrounded. Our refuge is supposedly between the Acero and Oro rivers.

The report seems to be diversionary.

Altitude = 2,000 meters.

From: *The Bolivian Diary* by Ernesto Che Guevara

"ONCE AGAIN I FEEL THE RIBS OF ROCINANTE BENEATH MY HEELS. ONCE MORE, I'M ON THE ROAD WITH THE SHIELD ON MY ARM."

ERNESTO CHE GUEVARA

FAREWELLS

Havana

Fidel,

At this moment I remember many things—when I met you in María Antonia's house [in Mexico], when you proposed I come along, all the tensions involved in the preparations [for the *Granma* expedition]. One day they came by and asked who should be notified in case of death, and the real possibility of that fact struck us all. Later we knew that it was true, that in a revolution one wins or dies (if it is a real one). Many comrades fell along the way to victory.

Today everything has a less dramatic tone, because we are more mature. But the event repeats itself. I feel that I have fulfilled the part of my duty that tied me to the Cuban revolution in its territory, and I say goodbye to you, to the comrades, to your people, who are now mine.

I formally resign my positions in the leadership of the party, my post as minister, my rank of commander, and my Cuban citizenship. Nothing legal binds me to Cuba. The only ties are of another nature — those that cannot be broken as can appointments to a post.

Recalling my past life, I believe I have worked with sufficient honesty and dedication to consolidate the revolutionary triumph. My only serious failing was not having had more confidence in you from the first moments in the Sierra Maestra, and not having understood quickly enough your qualities as a leader and a revolutionary.

I have lived magnificent days, and at your side I felt the pride of belonging to our people in the brilliant yet sad days of the Caribbean [missile] crisis. Seldom has a statesman been more brilliant than you in those days. I am also proud of having followed you without hesitation, identified with your way of thinking and of seeing and appraising dangers and principles.

Other nations of the world call for my modest efforts. I can do that which is denied you because of your responsibility at the head of Cuba, and the time has come for us to part.

I want it known that I do so with a mixture of joy and sorrow. I leave here the purest of my hopes as a builder and the dearest of my loved ones. And I leave a people who received me as a son. That wounds a part of my spirit. I carry to new battlefronts the faith that you taught me, the revolutionary spirit of my people, the feeling of fulfilling the most sacred of duties: to fight against imperialism wherever it may be. This comforts and heals the deepest wounds.

I state once more that I free Cuba from any responsibility, except that which stems from its example. If my final hour finds me under other skies, my last thought will be of this people and especially of you. I am thankful for your teaching, your example, and I will try to be faithful up to the final consequences of my actions.

I have always been identified with the foreign policy of our revolution, and I continue to be. Wherever I am, I will feel the responsibility of being a Cuban revolutionary, and I shall behave as such. I am not ashamed that I leave nothing material to my children and my wife; I am happy it is that way. I ask nothing for them, as the state will provide them with enough to live on and have an education.

I have a lot of things to say to you and to our people, but I feel they are unnecessary. Words cannot express what I would want them to, and I don't think it's worthwhile to keep scribbling away.

Hasta la victoria siempre! Patria o muerte!

I embrace you with all my revolutionary fervor.

Che

TO MY PARENTS 1965

Dear old folks,

Once again I feel the ribs of Rocinante beneath my heels. Once again, I'm on the road with my shield on my arm. Almost 10 years ago, I wrote you another farewell letter. As I recall, I lamented not being a better soldier and a better doctor. The latter no longer interests me; I am not such a bad soldier.

Nothing has changed in essence, except that I am much more conscious. My Marxism has taken root and become purified. I believe in armed struggle as the only solution for those peoples who fight to free themselves, and I am consistent with my beliefs. Many will call me an adventurer, and that I am—only one of a different sort: one who risks his skin to prove his truths.

It is possible that this may be the end. I don't seek it, but it's within the logical realm of probabilities. If it should be so, I send you a final embrace. I have loved you very much, only I have not known how to express my affection. I am extremely rigid in my actions, and I think that sometimes you did not understand me. It was not easy to understand me. Nevertheless, please believe me today.

Now a willpower that I have polished with an artist's delight will sustain some shaky legs and some weary lungs. I will do it.

Give a thought once in a while to this little soldier of fortune of the 20th century.

A kiss to Celia, to Roberto, Juan Martín and Patotín, to Beatriz, to everybody. For you, a big hug from your obstinate and prodigal son,

Ernesto

TO MY CHILDREN 1965

Dear Hildita, Aleidita, Camilo, Celia, and Ernesto,

If you ever have to read this letter, it will be because I am no longer with you. You will hardly remember me, and the smaller ones will not remember me at all.

Your father has been a man who acted on his beliefs and has certainly been loyal to his convictions.

Grow up as good revolutionaries. Study hard so that you can master technology, which allows us to master nature. Remember that the revolution is what is important, and each one of us, alone, is worth nothing.

Above all, always be capable of feeling deeply any injustice committed against anyone, anywhere in the world. This is the most beautiful quality in a revolutionary.

Until forever, my children. I still hope to see you. A great big kiss and a big hug from

Papá

TO MY CHILDREN
FROM SOMEWHERE IN BOLIVIA, 1966

My dearest Aliusha, Camilo, Celita and Tatico,

I write to you from far away and in great haste, which means I can't tell you about my latest adventures. It's a pity, because I've met some very interesting friends through Pepe the Crocodile [Uncle Sam]. Another time...

Right now I want to tell you that I love you all very much and I remember you always, along with mama, although the younger ones I almost only know through photos, as they were very tiny when I left. In a minute I'm going to get a photo taken so that you know how I look these days—a little bit older and uglier.

This letter should arrive about the time Aliusha has her sixth birthday, so may it serve to congratulate her and hope that she has a very happy birthday.

Aliusha, you should study hard and help your mother in everything you can. Remember, you are the oldest.

Camilo, you should swear less as in school you shouldn't speak like that and you have to learn what is appropriate. Celita, help your grandmother around the house as much as you can and continue being as sweet as when we said goodbye—do you remember? How could you not. Tatico, you should grow and become a man so that later we'll see what you make of yourself. If imperialism still exists, we'll set out to fight it. If it is finished, you, Camilo and I will take a vacation on the moon.

Give a kiss from me to your grandparents, to Miriam and her baby, to Estela and Carmita, and here's an elephant-sized kiss from...

Papá

[Note in the margin:]

To Hildita [Che's oldest daughter], another elephant-sized kiss and tell her I'll write soon, but now I don't have time

From: *Che Guevara Reader: Writings on Politics and Revolution* by Ernesto Che Guevara.

FURTHER READING

In collaboration with the Che Guevara Studies Center in Havana, headed by Che's widow, Aleida March, Ocean Press has initiated the Che Guevara publishing project to make available the complete writings of the legendary revolutionary to a new generation. This project includes new, authorized and corrected editions of some classic texts and the publication of several unpublished works by Che Guevara.

CHE GUEVARA IN HIS OWN WORDS INCLUDES:

CHE GUEVARA READER

SELF-PORTRAIT: A LITERARY AND PHOTOGRAPHIC MEMOIR

MOTORCYCLE DIARIES

REMINISCENCES OF THE CUBAN REVOLUTIONARY WAR

THE BOLIVIAN DIARY

GUERRILLA WARFARE

LATIN AMERICA: AWAKENING OF A CONTINENT

OUR AMERICA AND THEIRS

GLOBAL JUSTICE

CRITICAL NOTES ON POLITICAL ECONOMY

MARX & ENGELS: A BIOGRAPHICAL INTRODUCTION

These books are also available from Ocean Sur in Spanish

www.oceanbooks.com.au
www.oceansur.com

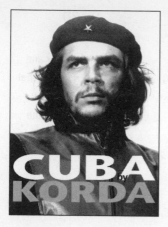

CUBA BY KORDA
Alberto Korda

If you don't know his name, you know his photograph of Che staring into the distance like a prophet, an image that has been reproduced on millions of T-shirts and posters around the world. This is the first publication of the work of the Cuban photographer Alberto Korda celebrated for his iconic photograph of Che Guevara. This book includes Korda's comments explaining the background to many of his incredible photos of the early years of the Cuban revolution.

ISBN 978-1-920888-64-0

MARX & ENGELS
A Biographical Introduction
Ernesto Che Guevara

A thoughtful introduction to the lives and work of Marx and Engels by a famous revolutionary practitioner, Che Guevara. This new, previously unpublished book makes an insightful contribution to the revival of interest in Marxism, and includes Che's reading list of essential Marxist classics.

ISBN 978-1-920888-92-3 (Also available in Spanish 978-1-921235-25-2)

OUR AMERICA AND THEIRS
Che, Kennedy and the Debate on Free Trade
Ernesto Che Guevara

To check the spread of revolution in Latin America after the Cuban revolution, US President John F. Kennedy initiated the "Alliance for Progress"—a program for free trade and development in the Americas. Che Guevara, representing the Cuban revolutionary government, condemned the plan as a new strategy to subjugate the continent to US interests.

ISBN 978-1-876175-96-2 (Also available in Spanish ISBN 978-1-920888-86-2)

CHE: A MEMOIR BY FIDEL CASTRO

Edited by David Deutschmann

For the first time Fidel Castro writes with candor and emotion about a historic revolutionary partnership that changed the face of Cuba and Latin America. Fidel vividly portrays Che—the man, the revolutionary, the intellectual—revealing much about his own inimitable determination and character.

ISBN 978-1-920888-25-1

(Also available in Spanish ISBN 978-1-921235-02-3)

TANIA

Undercover with Che Guevara in Bolivia

Ulises Estrada

Written by her Cuban compañero, Tania is a gripping account of the extraordinary woman who fought and died alongside Che Guevara in Bolivia. Tania was one of Cuba's most successful agents In Latin America, penetrating Bolivian high society and preparing the way for Che Guevara's clandestine entry into the country. When her cover was blown, Tania joined the guerrilla movement but was killed in an ambush in August 1967.

Tania is portrayed by Franka Potente in the movie CHE from Steven Soderbergh and Benicio Del Toro.

ISBN 978-1-876175-43-6 (Also available in Spanish ISBN 978-1-920888-21-3)

CHE GUEVARA AND THE LATIN AMERICAN REVOLUTION

Manuel "Barbarroja" Piñeiro

The organizer of Cuba's support for liberation movements, "Barbarroja" (Red Beard) makes some startling new revelations about Cuba's role in Latin America and offers some profound insights into Che Guevara's life and legacy.

ISBN 978-1-920888-46-6 (Also available in Spanish ISBN 978-1-920888-85-5)

SELF PORTRAIT
A PHOTOGRAPHIC AND LITERARY MEMOIR

ERNESTO CHE GUEVARA

ISBN 978-1-876175-82-5, 312 PP.

PHOTOS THROUGHOUT

A remarkable photographic and literary memoir offering an intimate look at the man behind the icon that draws on the rich seam of diaries, letters, poems, journalism, and short stories Che Guevara left behind him in Cuba.

This unique book was compiled in close collaboration with Che's family, using exclusive material from his family's private archives, revealing Che's personal world and unveiling his extraordinary candor, irony, dry wit and passion.

The photographs, taken from the Guevara family albums, bring to light a surprisingly sensitive and artistic edge to the legendary revolutionary. A dedicated amateur photographer, Che's own self-portraits are a stunning feature of this selection, much of which has never before been published.

"This beautiful, enlightening volume humanizes Che." —*Rain Taxi*

ALSO AVAILABLE IN SPANISH ISBN 978-1-876175-89-4

CHE GUEVARA READER
WRITINGS ON POLITICS AND REVOLUTION

ERNESTO CHE GUEVARA

ISBN 978-1-876175-69-6, 430 PP.

This bestselling anthology features the most complete selection of Che Guevara's writings, letters, and speeches available in English.

Recognized as one of *Time* magazine's "icons of the 20th Century," Ernesto Che Guevara became a legend in his own time and has now reemerged as a political symbol for a new generation of political activists.

More than just a guerrilla strategist, Che Guevara was a profound thinker who made a lasting contribution to revolutionary theory.

This Reader includes four sections: the Cuban revolutionary war (1956–58); the years in government in Cuba (1959–65); Che's views on the major international issues of the time, especially his vision of the Latin American revolution; and a selection of letters written by Che, including his farewell letters to Fidel Castro and his children and family.

ALSO AVAILABLE IN SPANISH ISBN 978-1-876175-93-1

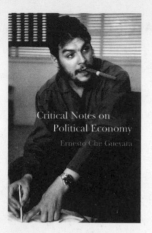

CRITICAL NOTES ON POLITICAL ECONOMY
A REVOLUTIONARY HUMANIST APPROACH TO MARXIST ECONOMICS

ERNESTO CHE GUEVARA

ISBN 978-1-876175-55-9, 300 PP.

The first publication in any language of Che Guevara's controversial and critical analysis of the Soviet economic model. As minister for industry, Che Guevara prepared this manuscript to compare (and contrast) Cuba's experience with that of the Soviet bloc. With extensive appendices, this is the complete anthology of Che Guevara's writings on political economy.

As a leading member of the revolutionary government in Cuba after 1959, Che Guevara was head of the Cuban National Bank. His simple signature of "Che" on Cuba's banknotes angered the heads of international banks and finance capital who considered it a denigration of the office. With these responsibilities Che was able to put into practice some of his ideas about how to achieve a transition from a capitalist economy to a socialist society.

ALSO AVAILABLE IN SPANISH ISBN 978-1-920888-63-3

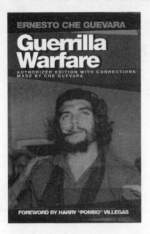

GUERRILLA WARFARE

ERNESTO CHE GUEVARA
FOREWORD BY
HARRY "POMBO" VILLEGAS

ISBN 978-1-920888-28-4 , 157 PP.

A bestselling classic for decades, this is Che Guevara's own incisive analysis of the Cuban revolution — a text studied by his admirers and adversaries alike. This is an account of what happened in Cuba and why, explaining how a small group of dedicated fighters grew in strength with the support of the Cuban people, overcoming their limitations to defeat a dictator's army.

This new edition features a revised translation and a foreword by Harry "Pombo" Villegas, Che's compañero in Bolivia and Africa, who was one of the few survivors of Che's Bolivian campaign.

"The positive feature of guerrilla warfare is that each guerrilla fighter is ready to die not just to defend an idea but to make that idea a reality."
—Ernesto Che Guevara

ALSO AVAILABLE IN SPANISH ISBN 978-1-920888-29-9

LATIN AMERICA
AWAKENING OF A CONTINENT

ERNESTO CHE GUEVARA

ISBN 978-1-920888-38-1, 400 PP.

The name Che Guevara is synonymous with Latin America. Here, for the first time in one volume, is a comprehensive overview of Che Guevara's unique perspective on the continent of Latin America, showing his cultural depth and rigorous intellect.

From his youthful travels throughout Latin America until his death in Bolivia, Che was a prodigious writer. In this classic selection of his journalism, essays, speeches, letters and poems, the reader can observe Che's development from spectator to participant in the struggles of the Americas, and finally to theoretician of the Latin American reality.

It features unpublished poems including *To the Bolivian Miners, My tears for you Guatemala* and *Spain in America;* unpublished articles including *Machu-Picchu: Enigmatic Stone of America, View from the Bank of the Greatest of Rivers, The Social Role of Doctors in Latin America* and *Workers of the United States: Friends or Enemies?* and excerpts from his first and last diaries.

ALSO AVAILABLE IN SPANISH ISBN 978-1-876175-71-9

MOTORCYCLE DIARIES
NOTES ON A LATIN AMERICAN JOURNEY

ERNESTO CHE GUEVARA
PREFACE BY ALEIDA GUEVARA

ISBN 978-1-876175-70-2 , 175 PP. + 24 PP. PHOTOS

ALSO AVAILABLE AS MOVIE TIE-IN EDITION:

978-1-920888-10-7

The book of the movie of the same name by Walter Salles, starring Gael García Bernal. The young Che Guevara's lively and highly entertaining travel diary features exclusive, unpublished photos taken by the 23-year-old Ernesto on his journey across a continent, and a tender preface by Aleida Guevara, offering an insightful perspective on her father—the man and the icon.

"It's about a journey of discovery that becomes one of self-discovery as well. It's about the emotional and political choices we all have to make in life. It's also about friendship, about solidarity. Finally, it's about finding one's place in the world—one that's worth fighting for."—Walter Salles, director of "The Motorcycle Diaries"

ALSO AVAILABLE IN SPANISH ISBN 978-1-920888-11-4

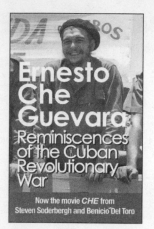

REMINISCENCES OF THE CUBAN REVOLUTIONARY WAR

ERNESTO CHE GUEVARA

PREFACE BY ALEIDA GUEVARA

ISBN 978-1-920888-33-6, 307 PP. + 32 PP. PHOTOS

Now the movie *CHE* from Steven Soderbergh and Benicio Del Toro

Part 1 (The Argentine) of Steven Soderbergh and Benicio Del Toro's movie is based on this book.

From 1956 to 1959, the people of Cuba struggled against immense odds to emerge victorious from years of brutal dictatorship, poverty, and corruption. *Reminiscences of the Cuban Revolutionary War* is Che Guevara's classic account of the popular war that transformed a nation, as well as Che himself—from troop doctor to world-famous revolutionary.

Featuring a preface by Che Guevara's daughter, Aleida Guevara, and a new translation with Che's own corrections incorporated into the text for the first time, this edition also contains extraordinary photographs of the period.

ALSO AVAILABLE IN SPANISH ISBN 978-1-920888-36-7

THE BOLIVIAN DIARY

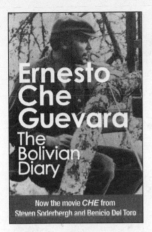

Now the movie *CHE* from
Steven Soderbergh and Benicio Del Toro

ERNESTO CHE GUEVARA

PREFACE BY CAMILO GUEVARA

INTRODUCTION BY FIDEL CASTRO

ISBN 978-1-920888-24-4 , 307 PP. + 32 PP. PHOTOS

Part 2 (Guerrilla) of Steven Soderbergh and Benicio Del Toro's movie about Che Guevara is based on this book.

"Thanks to Che's invariable habit of noting the main events of each day, we have rigorously exact, priceless, and detailed information on the heroic final months of his life in Bolivia." —Fidel Castro

This is Che Guevara's famous last diary, found in his backpack when he was captured by the Bolivian Army in October 1967. It became an instant international bestseller.

Newly revised, with a preface by Che's eldest son Camilo and extraordinary unpublished photos, this is the definitive, authorized edition of the diary, which after his death catapulted Che to iconic status throughout the world.

ALSO AVAILABLE IN SPANISH ISBN 978-1-920888-30-5

"IF YOU TREMBLE WITH INDIGNATION AT EVERY INJUSTICE THEN YOU ARE A COMRADE OF MINE."

ERNESTO CHE GUEVARA

¡HASTA LA VICTORIA SIEMPRE!